MINIMALISM MADE SIMPLE

BY

SIMON DAVIES

Text Copyright © Simon Davies

All rights reserved. No part of this guide may be reproduced in any form without permission in writing from the publisher except in the case of brief quotations embodied in critical articles or reviews.

Legal & Disclaimer

The information contained in this book and its contents is not designed to replace or take the place of any form of medical or professional advice; and is not meant to replace the need for independent medical, financial, legal or other professional advice or services, as may be required. The content and information in this book have been provided for educational and entertainment purposes only.

The content and information contained in this book have been compiled from sources deemed reliable, and it is accurate to the best of the Author's knowledge, information, and belief. However, the Author cannot guarantee its accuracy and validity and cannot be held liable for any errors and/or omissions. Further, changes are periodically made to this book as and when needed. Where appropriate and/or necessary, you must consult a professional (including but not limited to your doctor, attorney, financial advisor or such other professional advisor) before using any of the suggested remedies, techniques, or information in this book.

Upon using the contents and information contained in this book, you agree to hold harmless the Author from and against any damages, costs, and expenses, including any legal fees potentially resulting from the application of any of the information provided by this book. This disclaimer applies to any loss, damages or injury caused by the use and application, whether directly or indirectly, of any advice or information presented, whether for breach of contract, tort, negligence, personal injury, criminal intent, or under any other cause of action.

You agree to accept all risks of using the information presented inside this book.

You agree that by continuing to read this book, where appropriate and/or necessary, you shall consult a professional (including but not limited to your doctor, attorney, or financial advisor or such other advisor as needed) before using any of the suggested remedies, techniques, or information in this book.

Table of Contents

Minimalist Living Made Easy

Introduction 1

Chapter 1: What is Minimalism and How it All Started...........................2

   1.1 What Is Minimalism Living, What Does It Entail 3

   1.2 What is the purpose of minimalism? 6

Chapter 2: Are you a Minimalist? 8

   2.1 What does it mean to be a minimalist? 9

   2.2 Common Misconceptions about Minimalism 13

Chapter 3: Dealing with Clutter in Life 15

   3.1 How Decluttering Changes Your Life 17

Chapter 4: Minimalism in Different Areas of Life 19

   4.1 Essential Relationship 19

   4.2 Parenting 24

   4.3 Career Life 26

   4.4 Finances 30

Chapter 5: Needs & Wants 32

   5.1 What is the difference between things you need & things you want 33

   5.2 How To Identify the Thing You Need From Things You Want 34

   5.3 How to Distinguish the Differences between the Two that Promote Minimalism..35

Chapter 6: Optimizing Life for Minimalism 37
6.1 A Simple Plan for Home Declutter 38
6.2 Decluttering Your Home 40
6.3 Decluttering Your Material Possessions 49
6.4 Decluttering your Gadgets 53
6. 5 Decluttering Your Schedule 58
Chapter 7: A life of Abundance 65
Chapter 8: Minimalism Maintenance 69
8.1 Ways to Maintain Your Minimalist Lifestyle Permanently 70
8.2 Common Items to Never Buy If You Want to Have a Clutter-Free Home 73
8.3 Fighting the desire 75
Conclusion 76

The Minimalist Budget Made Easy

Introduction 79

Chapter 1: What is a Minimalist? 81

    1.1 Why Less Is More 82

    1.2 Signs You Be A Minimalist In The Making 85

Chapter 2: A Minimalist's Approach to Money 87

    2.1 What the Minimalist Budget Is Not 88

    2.2 Minimalist Living vs. Frugal Living 88

    2.3 How to Be More Frugal and More of A Minimalist 90

    2.4 Guide to Spending Money as a Minimalist 91

    2.5 Intention over Restriction 97

    2.6 The 50/30/20 Rule of Budgeting 98

Chapter 3: Avoiding Unnecessary Spending 102

    3.1 The Psychology of Spending Money 102

    3.2 How to Differentiate Compulsive from Excessive Spending 105

    3.3 Effective Ways to Overcome Overspending 106

    3.4 Importance of Budgeting 107

Chapter 4: Creating an Effective Budget 110

    4.1 7 Ways to Save Money with Minimalism 117

    4.2 Steps to Having an Effective Minimalist Budget 119

Chapter 5: Budgeting for the Long Term 130

Chapter 6: Setting Your Financial Goals 133

Chapter 7: Dealing with that Dreaded Debt 135

7.1 Using the Concept of Minimalism to Plan Your Personal Transformation 137

7.2 Mistakes to Avoid When Dealing With Debt 139

7.3 Effective Strategies to Clear Debts 141

Chapter 8: Valuing Time 143

8.1 Time vs. Money 143

8.2 How to Work Smarter Not Harder 145

8.3 Why Society Doesn't Value Time 146

8.4 Busy vs. Productive 149

8.5 Productivity and Minimalism 151

Conclusion 154

MINIMALIST LIVING MADE EASY

By Simon Davies

INTRODUCTION

The truth is, no one wakes up and says, "Oh, I want to start a minimalist lifestyle starting today." No one simply falls for it. For many, it takes years and losing good relationships and career before they realize that there is a toxic in their life they needed to get rid of.

This was the case for me.

For years, I let my life out of control, which affected my relationship, my career, and even social life negatively – everything seemed so rampant. I know it was my fault; everything was just a result of my own doing. But it came to a point that I had enough – every bad thing must come to an end.

When I discovered minimalism lifestyle, I was able to turn my life around and direct it to a more organized, pleasant life.

Anyone can live a minimalist life. I believe that your life is not set in stone and anyone can improve or change. All the choices and decisions you make about the quality of your life are laid out based on the simplicity or complexity of your decisions.

In this book, I want to share how life-changing minimalism can be and how to do it right. And hopefully, it can help you take back control over your life and direct you to the path of contentment.

Furthermore, this book is also meant to help you develop new skills and discover hobbies that you didn't think you would like. Basically, you will learn the basics of having fun and enjoying life for what it really has to offer. This will also help you become more appreciative of the basics of living, without unnecessary expensive materialistic things, which frees up your mind, and lets you find your purpose and eventually, allows you to become a calmer, happier, and more loving individual.

I hope you enjoy this audiobook, the only thing I ask is if you could please leave an honest review after listening, thanks

Chapter 1

What is Minimalism and How it All Started

It has been long debated within the design community as to when exactly, minimalism first came about. Some people believe that it all started in the middle of the Modernist movement during the early 20th century when new materials like steel, glass, and concrete were starting to become widely available. On the other hand, some argue that it really started much later, as an extension of the Minimalist art movement during the 1960s to 1970s, when artists like Ellsworth Kelly and Donald Judd turned back from Abstract Expressionism supporting next level abstractions which includes simple geometric shapes.

In spite of its blurred timeline, minimalism has been – and continues to be –one of the most powerful movements of the 20th and 21st centuries throughout the world of architecture, art, product design, and lifestyle. A response against excess, the goal of this Zen-like approach is to show the beauty of simplicity, elegance, and utility by getting rid of things that might be unnecessary.

Today, minimalism is usually associated with Japanese traditional Zen-style design and home organization approach (thanks to Marie Kondo's show on Netflix that influenced many all over the world to discard any item in their home that does not "spark joy"). Zen style design and art focus on getting rid of any unnecessary add-ons or decorations. These arts are usually referred to as aesthetics of elimination as they allow endless beauty and profusion occur from less, instead of more. Huge creative power is used into recognizing and eliminating all unnecessary things, whether it is an element, space, shapes, colour, decoration, and even habits.

1.1 What Is Minimalism Living, What Does It Entail

Just like on many other "trends" it's quite unfortunate that a lot of people go all-out towards being minimalist, even if they actually have no idea what a minimalist lifestyle truly entails. For some, living a minimalist lifestyle means living in an isolated place. And while for others, it could mean living a luxurious life.

What is it really about?

Have you ever had an empty cupboard or cabinet space in your home? Chances are you have had the urge to find or even buy something you can put in it to just fill it up and give it a "purpose." But have you really given enough thought if the thing you are going to put in it has a purpose? While your cupboard or cabinet space is there for a reason, it shouldn't be necessary to use them unless you really needed to. Do you really need to buy a dozen piece of tableware even if you live alone just to fill in your cupboard? Or do you really need to buy that swan figurine just to have something to put on your cabinet display space? Those are just unnecessary clutters!

Living a minimalist lifestyle means living only with things you really use and need. This is not to say that becoming a minimalist means having to spend less money; this simply means living a life that makes you spend money only on things that you actually need.

Aside from having a lot of unnecessary things, a lot of people lack contentment in life. Wanting to attain success quickly would not guarantee the happiness you might be looking for; it would rather continue to make life a lot harder than what it already is.

Living a minimalist lifestyle involves being content with how your life already is as long as you're healthy and your basic needs are met. But this doesn't mean it's unnecessary to want a better life, a better body, or a better job – there's always room for improvement, you don't have to be unhappy just because you haven't had the better version of yourself or your life just yet.

A lot of people find it difficult to be content, maybe because it's so easy to compare your life to others', which can be really toxic. Living a minimalist life, on the other hand, is focusing on what you already have and making the best out of it.

It takes time

Being a successful minimalist takes a huge amount of change in your life, as well as routine and your way of thinking.

While a lot of people associate minimalism with reducing the number of your possessions, it's just not about that. In fact, minimalism is more about reducing the things that are holding you back, things that consume a lot of your time, which make you inefficient on a regular basis.

Minimalism also has something to do with a change of mindset. It's a lot more about the individual, the feelings, and experiences rather than about your physical possessions.

It is the process of changing your life entirely that takes time and is not just about getting rid of your things in your house. It is a process that involves accepting and knowing that many things are essentially holding you back.

It shows how spending more of your time with people and enduring different experiences rather than shopping and spending money will have more of an incredible effect on your life. Unlike some fundamental life-changing courses or methods, the benefits you will get from minimalism may take some time to take effect and become obvious. But then again, trusting the process is a part of the whole idea of minimalism.

MINIMALISM IS INTENTIONALITY

It's marked by purpose, clarity, as well as intentionality. At its very core, minimalism is the intentional highlighting of the things that are important to us and the elimination of the stuff that distracts us from it. It's a lifestyle that attracts intentionality. And therefore, it attracts improvements in most parts of your life.

MINIMALISM IS FREEDOM FROM PHYSICAL POSSESSIONS

Today's culture has made us believe that a good life can be found by accruing things – by having as many things as we can. Many of us think that the more things we have, the better, which gives us this kind of idea that happiness can be bought at a shopping store.

But having a good life is not about having more things.

Minimalism helps us have freedom from the all-consuming desire to possess everything. It drags us off consumerism and encourages us to seek happiness elsewhere. It helps us give importance to experiences, relationships, healthcare, and soul-care.

MINIMALISM IS FREEDOM FROM MODERN HYSTERIA

We live in a feverish pace of life. Many of us seem to be rushed, hurried, and stressed. We tend to work at passionate hours just to pay the bill as if working is the only thing we are meant to do. We rush to doing one activity to another or even multitasking while doing so, but at the end of the day, still not finding the satisfaction of getting things done. We keep ourselves in close connection with others through the internet, but real life-changing relationships carry on eluding us.

Minimalism helps us slow our life down and keeps us free from this modern mania to live faster. It gives us the opportunity to find the freedom to disengage. It seeks to highlight only life's essentials. It pursues to get rid of the frivolous and keep the only things that are important. And throughout the process, it values the intentional undertakings that overall, add value to life.

MINIMALISM IS FREEDOM FROM DECEPTION

Even though no one purposely chooses it, a lot of us live in deception. We live one life with our family, one with our co-workers, and another one with our neighbors. The lifestyle we have requires us to render a specific external image depending on the situation.

On the other hand, a simple life is ruled by unity and consistency. It is a form of lifestyle that's entirely transferable regardless of what the situation is. This means not looking at Friday night and Monday morning differently.

MINIMALISM IS COUNTER-CULTURAL

We live in a society that is heavily influenced by celebrities. We see them on TV, read about them in magazines, and even follow them on social media. Their lives are envied by many, and many wish they lived the same way these celebrities do. People who are living a minimalist lifestyle are not impressed by the media correspondingly. A minimalist doesn't fit into the culture of consumerism that's endorsed by corporations and influential people. Yet, they're living a life that's pretty inviting and attractive.

While a lot of people are racing to acquire glamour, success, and reputation, minimalism can be recognized with a quieter, smaller, and calmer voice. It encourages us to consume less, slow down, and enjoy more.

MINIMALISM IS COMPLETELY ACHIEVABLE

Anyone can be a minimalist. As long as you are open to embracing an intentional lifestyle of living with less and leave your old lifestyle forever, you can be successful at it.

1.2 What is the purpose of minimalism?

A minimalist lifestyle is a life that demands the best of it by getting rid of the things that instead of making your life fun and fulfilling, making it more difficult and miserable.

Today, more and more people are starting to see the rewards they can get if they choose to live with less stuff. But again, what you have to keep in mind is that minimalism is not about being cheap or compromising your basic comforts for the sake of some principled religious philosophy. It is not even close to that. It is simply a choice fortified by the desire to reduce your possessions and to choose to live a simpler life with simpler intention.

You no longer want to be part of the dizzying rat-race of the 21st century's consumer world. Many people may have different definitions of minimalism, but the main idea of this lifestyle is to help you. Here are some of the things you can do when looking to change to a minimalist lifestyle:

- Be free from excess stuff
- Chase your passions
- Contribute beyond yourself
- Create more and consume less
- Determine your missions
- Discover your life purpose
- Eliminate your dissatisfaction
- Experience freedom
- Pay attention to your health
- Grow as a person
- Live in the moment
- Make the most of your time

By following the minimalist lifestyle, you will be able to finally find lasting happiness – and isn't that what each one of us is looking for? All of us want to be happy and most of us think that having everything – power, material things, recognition, etc. – is what going to make us truly happy. The purpose of minimalism is to help us realize these things are worthless if seen from the perspective of someone who knows what genuine happiness feels like.

Chapter 2

ARE YOU A MINIMALIST?

What makes minimalist individuals different from those who are not? Here are some typical signs or traits you may develop as you live your life following the minimalist lifestyle.

You see depth within simplicity

Within every item that you have, the experiences you get, and even with people you meet, you will start to see an underlying emphasis on their functionality and purpose. It's like when you look at something, the first thought you have is "This can be very useful for me," instead of "This will look good in my living room."

You see organizing every part of your life with a therapeutic appeal

You either live a ploddingly well-ordered life or aspire to be. Making a list is something you love to do: must-do lists, grocery lists, goal lists, all the lists! As soon as you thought of an idea or a plan, you immediately feel empowered, and even the hardest tasks seem to be doable.

You seek for everything to look good together all the time, but you don't make a fuss about your looks

Unless you have been invited to a party, you're likely not to be seen dressed up to the nines. No matter what the occasion is, you'd always rather comfortable clothing and look natural. Again, simplicity is what you live for.

You appreciate quality and the finer things, and get little to no satisfaction from cheaper alternatives

While you might still think that it's a good idea to save some money, you'd rather be spending $500 on a high-quality appliance that may last for years, instead of buying a $50 one that even though may look exactly the same, you cannot guarantee the quality of it. You have a great appreciation for fine quality and craftsmanship and you feel the more of a purpose it has, the better.

You find cleanliness and functionality more appealing than the overly decorative

Your space is more valued and you'd prefer sit on the floor like how Japanese people would instead of filling up every inch of your house with things that don't have any functionality and purpose. This is not to say that your home is expected to be dull and lacking in personality. In fact, for many, it's the other way around – it simply means that you choose all your stuff carefully. Your home becomes an evident extension of your personality.

Cleaning becomes a hobby for you rather than a chore

It becomes a norm for you to pick out things that are not in their right places and put them where they should be in the first place. Clearing out the superfluous brings you a sense of fulfillment as well as simplifying your life and re-evaluating your priorities.

Your loathing to clutter extends to the people you encounter every day

You are very picky about whom you spend your time with and the people you interact with. So, you probably find yourself cleaning out your Facebook friend list from time to time as well!

Like many popular "*trends*", there are going to be inadequate knockoffs that don't hold up the values of a successful minimalist. On the other hand, once these traits are applied systematically and considerately, this lifestyle can leave you with powerful lasting benefits that go beyond sheer visuals.

2.1 What does it mean to be a minimalist?

Regardless of the hype around minimalism, it's quite obvious that many people still get a wrong impression of it. Again, it's not just about limiting the number of your possessions and living far from the comfort offered by the modern world.

And while such extreme forms of minimalism do exist, there are much milder forms of this lifestyle, some of which that still provide all the benefits a minimalist life can bring but doesn't require you to sell all the things you own and live in a 90-square-foot box in the middle of nowhere. Minimalism is by no means a radical change of lifestyle, but instead an optimal one.

Minimalism isn't a set of rules.

Because there are no strict rules you have to follow, the idea of minimalism may come in different for different people. For some, it might only be about getting rid of physical possessions and decluttering their homes, while for others, it is more about getting rid of unnecessary thoughts, beliefs, and even people.

To illustrate this diversity, we asked different people living a minimalist life to explain what minimalism means for them.

"For me, minimalism is living deliberately and considerately of the environment, ourselves, and those around us. It means removing (and then not re-accumulating) things in life that we don't use or need. In my life, that means ridding myself of the "stuff" of life that begins to accumulate and overwhelm me, being intentional about purchases, and diminishing waste and clutter." —**Mary Spires (Accountant)**

"Minimalism is my rebellion against consumerism. I'm tired of buying things because I'm *supposed* to have the latest new style or makeup trend. I want to save money and only buy what I truly love or need. I never want to go into debt like my parents did. It makes me feel calmer and more in tune with what I actually own instead of feeling ingratitude." —**Lilly Sander (Librarian)**

"Being able to let go... not just of things but of associating things with people and memories. After being an only child, the oldest granddaughter, and only great-granddaughter/granddaughter to have any children on my side... everything has been passed down to me for my kids, apparently. At 35, I am the matriarch of the family and the only one with children to carry in our family. So, what? It means everything is now in my home and basement that was my family owned. I have had to take baby steps to let it go. I'm only starting this journey. The courier cabinet that my grandfather made my grandmother 100 years ago for their first wedding anniversary... my grandmother's hope chest... my mother's wedding dress... I am having a hard time letting it all go but piece by piece, I am coming to terms that the stuff is not my mother, grandmother, and great grandmother... I will keep some of it, but I honor them every day being a good mom to my 3 young children, not by stashing their stuff away in my basement." — *Elizabeth Kerns (Teacher)*

"For me, minimalism is item curation. I feel like I don't see minimalists writing enough about how cool and valuable stuff can be. Stuff gets a bad rap in minimalism. I like buying things. I like researching things to buy. I like thinking of ways that I can buy something cool and unique to replace one or a couple of the things I already own. I obsess over stuff. If you have just the right stuff, you don't need any other stuff. I have 5 shirts, 3 pants, a pair of jeans, and 6 shirts. Each and every piece was lovingly picked out and I have fun picking them out. It seems like most people achieve minimalism by caring about things less. I achieved it by caring about things more. Minimalism is a hobby for me. Yes, it takes time and effort to curate a beautiful list of objects, but it takes time and effort to practice any hobby." —*Ricky Manning (Mathematician)*

"I think everyone is different, it is a lifestyle that adapts to you and your needs. There is no 'one size fits all' approach to minimalism. We are a family of four that travel worldwide full time, world schooling our kids as we go, being able to really immerse ourselves in new cultures and languages. We are a family of minimalists, we have one carry on size suitcase each and that is all. We have what we need, we have clothes, depending on the country depends on what we have; we spent 18 months in hot and sunny countries so we only had short stops. This winter we went where there was snow, so we had thermals, jumpers, and coats. I think the key for us is not holding onto things that we do not need. When we change climates, we change what we own; the kids outgrow their clothes each season which makes this easier. We do not get too attached to the 'stuff' because that is all it is 'stuff' – things that can be replaced. Our adventures and experiences, time spent together creating memories, that is what living is all about. We have all our toiletries, we have our devices, a couple phones, a couple laptops as we work remotely online, and a couple kindles for our children as they LOVE to read, and books are SO heavy. The children have a few toys each and a favorite teddy. When we are going to be choosing a place for a few months we buy extras for the kids, in Costa Rica we had a pool, so we bought some cool inflatable pool toys while we there. When we leave we leave them for the next guests. In France, we bought a pop-up beach tent and a football, again when we left we left that for the next guests. We are not attached to things like we (the parents) used to be. Before we made this transition, we had a four-bedroom farmhouse by the beach and we had SO MUCH 'stuff' we had two kids' rooms and a playroom full of stuff, I had two wardrobes with ten/fifteen years' worth of clothes in – clothes that didn't even fit anymore? Things I was just holding on to? I think it is definitely a process, both physically and mentally. When we started clearing out, I was emotional about it; I had attached so much emotion to all these things. Toys the kids had played with and outgrown clothes I wore for certain events in my life. Things bought for us by people we cared about. The process for me really cleared so much mental baggage I was holding onto that I was not even aware of. It left me feeling so free and empowered. The kid's attitudes are abundance, they never feel lacking or without, and they are great at sharing. This makes us so happy, as many 'people' shared their fears and opinions about our kids' future issues, of not having 'stuff'. We have all we need and that is enough. I would highly recommend this lifestyle to others, maybe not as drastically as us we do not even have a home, but to get rid of the excess of 'stuff' people have and never use. When you are minimalists, it frees so much, space physically and mentally. As entrepreneurs, it cleared our minds and allowed us the mind freedom to create and grow into the leaders we needed to be to create our incredible businesses." —*Laura Helen (Forever Family Forever Free Blog)*

2.2 Common Misconceptions about Minimalism

When you tell someone that you're a "minimalist," they might immediately assume that you're a clean freak who goes ballistic over mess. But as mentioned earlier, it's way more than that. Now, let's expose all the common misconceptions about minimalism.

1. You Must Give Up Comfort and Convenience

Many people get intimidated by this lifestyle because they often think that it requires you to give up your belongings that give you your comfort on a daily basis. But you have to keep in mind that minimalism isn't about what you give up; instead, it's about what you keep. It's about keeping the things that carry value in your life and getting rid of the things that are holding you back from a more comfortable and pleasant life.

But for the sake of argument, then yes, okay… there are some minimalists who only have a couple of clothing items. But for most, the general rule is to focus on quality over quantity.

2. You Must Live Like a Monk

While most monks live following a minimalist lifestyle, it doesn't mean you have to be a monk and leave everything behind and live in a secluded place. While it's true that there are extreme minimalists who become monks, and vice versa, it's not necessary.

3. You Must Count Your Belongings

Although some minimalists would rather count the number of belongings they have, many minimalists don't which is perfectly fine. Many minimalists don't like to stick to a certain number because, for them, the number is not what's important – they prioritize on the fact that the things they own bring purpose or value to their like.

4. You Must Become Vegan and Live Zero Waste

Because minimalism is considered to be an alternative way of life, it's not surprising how it's still far from the mainstream. Similarly, living a sustainable lifestyle or being a minimalist is also considered an alternative lifestyle. This means that not because both lifestyles have something in common, it automatically means that one incorporates the other. The same way goes to living a zero waste lifestyle.

5. You Must Always Choose to Save Money

Another common misconception many people have about minimalism is that people who live by its principles are cheap. It's actually the other way around. As mentioned earlier, most minimalists make sure that they can get the very best of something, usually, disregarding the price tag. For example, if a minimalist person needs to buy a blender, he or she has to make sure that they can buy the best quality they can get. For a minimalist, it's better to buy something that is pricier as long as he can assure that he will be able to use it for years, instead of buying something that is very cheap but is expected to be disposed of after a few months of use. Rather than cheap people, it's more appropriate to label them as smart shoppers.

6. It Is all About Decluttering

This is no doubt the most common misconception about minimalism. For many people, a minimalist lifestyle is a synonym to decluttering. But the truth is that decluttering is simply a tool that is used to clear away the stuff that doesn't bring happiness or fulfillment into your life, in order for you to be able to focus better on things that do. While you can look at decluttering as a metaphor for ending something, decluttering on its own does not make you a minimalist as minimalism is a way of life, not a one-time action.

Minimalism lifestyle is not as intimidating as most people think it is. It doesn't restrict you to live a comfortable life. Instead, its goal is to give you a better life by highlighting things you should give more importance to.

Chapter 3

DEALING WITH CLUTTER IN LIFE

Clutter is a common challenge for many. This is known to keep you from being productive both from your work as well as personal life. Cluttered spaces are due to things not having their proper places, people shopping without a list or buying impulsively, being unable to decide whether or not you want to keep something because of its value.

These are usually surface reasons that cause clutter. However, the real reasons for clutter lie behind the surface and are connected to us physically and mentally. Regardless of how much paper or belongings you have, your clutter reflects who you are.

You are not able to clear the clutter by focusing on your belongings. How many times did you eliminate the clutter on your table or the pile of clothes next to your closet only to have it come back after a couple of days, making you feel like it's just impossible to get rid of the clutter? If this is something you experience on a regular basis, then it's possible that there's something else going on in the background that holds you back from letting go of it.

When you see beyond your physical clutter, you can then start to see its connection to your body and mind. So, how is your clutter connected to our physical body? Clutter can cause a lot of negative effects on the body including the following:

- × A study shows that over-consumption of stuff is linked to over-consumption of food
- × Aggravates allergies by promoting the buildup of dust mites, mold, dander, and other allergens
- × Creates a haven for germs
- × Delays you to do important tasks as it makes things hard to find

- × Increases risk of injuries
- × Its overwhelming presence drains your energy

Now let's take a look at how clutter affects one's mental perspective. Clutter is being accumulated in physical spaces once mental clutter starts to accumulate. The mental clutter is usually caused by stress, associated emotions, and small to big changes in life. When we are mentally cluttered, we find it hard to focus and often feeling mentally drained and heavy. The way we think usually represents how our physical environment looks like. Here are the ways clutter affects our mental health:

- × Abates your ability to make a decision
- × Escalates anxiety and stress
- × Inhibits you from living in the moment
- × Makes procrastination worse
- × Represses good things from getting into your life
- × Worsens symptoms of paruresis

By being aware of what goes on below the surface, it is going to be easier for you to do something about it. The plan of attack you will have will also affect your lifestyle changes on the whole. Once you clear up the clutter, it will affect different areas of your life. For example, once you get rid of the clutter in your room, you will be more motivated to do your task of the day and you will have one less thing to worry about which lowers the level of anxiety.

This also works the other way around. For example, when you are mentally and physically better, it gives you more motivation to declutter. So, before rolling your sleeves up and begin decluttering your space, take a look at it a little bit deeper and ask yourself, *how does my physical and mental state affect my environment?* Your mental and physical clutter presents the clutter in your environment. One of the best ways to getting rid of the clutter once and for all is determined by you.

3.1 How Decluttering Changes Your Life

It Keeps the Flow of Energy

All things around us, including ourselves, are made of energy, and getting rid of clutter is effective in boosting your energy levels. Energy has to flow without restrictions, but when there's something blocking the way, it inhibits the flow of energy. Just try it. Do you have a room or space in your house that you wanted to be clean but due to certain circumstances, you can't find the time or the motivation to clean it? Just clean it and see how your energy changes. After the little makeover you give to your space, you will be rewarded with neatness, clarity, and of course, more space.

It Saves You Time

Is frantically running around looking for things you can't find a normal scenario for you? How many times has trying to look for your keys or wallet made you late for work? Having a lot of stuff means having a lot of things to manage. Similarly, having less stuff makes it much easier for you to manage things, which means whenever you need something it will always be easier to find.

It Improves Your Mood

No matter how big or small the space you declutter or organize is, it will always boost your mood. A decluttered place feels like a safe place. This is beneficial for those who are suffering from anxiety and this is very obvious in people suffering from Obsessive Compulsive Disorder. For individuals who obsessively clean, organize, or count things, being in that "safe place" makes them calmer – even just temporarily. And while this is an extreme example, people with other clinical disorders may benefit from it also.

It Gives You a Chance to Help Those Who Are In Need

By decluttering, you're not only helping yourself, but you can also help people who are less fortunate. Imagine doing something that is beneficial for you not only physically and mentally, but also spiritually! Some of the best things to donate are clothes, books, and toys.

It Teaches Children How to Be Appreciative

If you're a parent who wants to practice minimalism, note that there's nothing wrong with giving nice things to your kids, given you have financial means to do so. But you must also keep in mind that there should be a fine line between enough and too much. By letting your kids have too many things may teach them to be hoarders. You should be careful; otherwise, they may turn out to be spoiled. Instead of appreciating it when you give them a toy, feeling of expectation is likely what they may feel.

It Encourages Us to Deal with Emotional Problems That May Be Triggering the Clutter

As mentioned earlier, just like how physical clutter can generate emotional problems, clutter can also be due to an unaddressed emotional clutter. Whether it is a problem with your relationship, job, or habits, clutter can be a mask for life dissatisfaction. Once you make a move in getting rid of your clutter, these emotional problems have a chance to surface and there will be a space to address your unhappiness.

It Opens Up New Opportunities

Imagine living your life without clutter. You will have more time to spend on things that truly matter to you. The way you approach life will change. Your self-esteem towards your relationship and social circle will improve. You can save more money and work towards your career growth. You will have more energy to spark creativity. By throwing away the unnecessary things in your life, more doors surely open for new and great opportunities – emotionally, physically, and spiritually.

Chapter 4

Minimalism in Different Areas of Life

After discovering the different aspects of this lifestyle, it didn't take long for me to realize how the benefits of minimalism are starting to affect each aspect of my life and not just my household.

Before this, I had a delusional description of minimalism. I, just like many people do, imagine people wearing capsule wardrobes with monochrome shades, a suitcase of clothes, or spectacularly simple-looking home with Scandinavian-inspired interiors. You have probably seen a lot of pictures dotted all over social media which make minimalism look like a lifestyle that only individuals with extreme self-discipline and a repugnance to shopping can be successful at.

At first glance, the minimalism lifestyle can be seen as superficial. The outwardly endless clear countertops and succulent plants in every corner of the room, and ever-diminishing closet seen on Instagram posts could be like and follower miners for some of those so-called *influencers* on social media. But there's a huge chance that they only embrace the idea of minimalism due to its aesthetic appeal.

This is not to say that there's something wrong with it. But this is to say that it could be deeper than that. Minimalism, for many who practices it, brings drastic changes to their life. The lifestyle is not only about how it can affect you visually or mentally, but it can also be about how it can affect every corner of your life.

4.1 Essential Relationship

First, let's talk about how minimalism can positively affect your relationships. The first way is that it encourages you to cut out unnecessary relationships, especially the toxic ones.

These relationships could be with a friend or a coworker that doesn't bring value to your life. Perhaps, they are rude to you or have a bad attitude. Perhaps, they have judged you or didn't show you respect. If there are people that are like this – may it be your romantic partner or relatives – minimalism can help you highlight the only things or people that you need in your life.

Minimalism can also help you realize that it's only you who control all the things you bring in to your life.

By adopting this mindset, you can learn how to live your life with purpose and commitment and help you accept the fact that some people that don't make you happy or make you unhappy should be let go once and for all.

Dating

By adopting minimalism to your dating life, you can start with zero and simply add on what's necessary to your relationship. This means giving him or her, the only things he or she needs – not anything unnecessary.

So, what am I talking about? These are the qualities that a relationship needs to make it stronger. These qualities include, but not limited to being:

- ❖ supportive
- ❖ accepting for who the person is
- ❖ ambitious to attaining his goals
- ❖ fun to be with

You can also seek these qualities when finding a person to be in a relationship with. This means removing the need to find someone who is 6-foot tall, has a fancy car or lives in a huge apartment.

If you choose to approach the dating scene the other way around, with a long list of "standards", you may end up accepting the wrong ones and overseeing the things that are more essential. "Yeah, he does work so hard and spends 80 hours at work, and has a luxury car."

This is not something that may likely benefit your life in the long run.

Applying minimalism on your dating approach may help you stay grounded. But of course, this is when you're ready to be serious and thinking about settling in already.

The truth is no one can tick off all the boxes on the list you might have put up. The only way you can check off all the boxes is if you list the small qualities that are deeper than material or superficial things.

There are many relationships that face fights and problems due to trivial things. Social media, unmet expectations, not saying things the right way, not reading the other person's mind, and even financial state can be trivial when you really dwell on the things that are more important in life. Minimalism helps us overlook those pointless things and just see the bigger picture.

Minimalism constantly reminds us of the positive sides of letting go. Just like how it restricts our attachments with certain objects in our lives, it also restricts us from routines and persons.

Stronger Marriage

I just celebrated my sixth wedding anniversary, which also happens to be approximately my second year of following a minimalist lifestyle. The two are closely related in my life.

A couple of months before my wedding, I experience a mild panic attack. No, I didn't think about running away or ditching my then soon-to-be wife. The attack happened when a moment of clarity sunk in and I realized that I had to get my expenses under control or it could lead to some serious issue in my marriage. I sat on the computer and started listing my debts against my assets. I didn't get positive results. Right that very moment, I promised myself to only buy something if I really need them.

This was before I even heard anything about minimalism and I definitely hadn't applied the idea of it on anything that I am aware of. But then, there I was, telling myself over and over again to spend less money in order to have better married life. From then on, I have become increasingly devoted to following the lifestyle and up to this day, it has continued to be beneficial to my married life in a lot of ways.

Here are some ways minimalism has helped me and my spouse build and keep a stronger marriage:

Better control of our finances

There's no denying the divorce rate is still soaring, and it's also a known fact that financial problems are one of the main reasons for it. When the couple is open to each other when it comes to finances from the beginning of the relationship, there will be higher chances for them to have a successful, lasting relationship.

A relationship that follows minimalism may likely have a plan on how and where they spend their income, no matter how much it is. While there is no rule on how and where you spend the money, many minimalist couples try to spend less than what they make.

Honest communication

Being able to calmly and openly talk about money is not easy for many couples. But once they figure out how to do it, most aspects of the relationship become easier.

For me personally, I like thinking of my relationship with my wife as an open-source project. Every part of our relationship is transparent and anything can be discussed. From minimalism, I learned the importance of examining and acknowledging some of the less positive parts of myself and make a proper adjustment before they lead to serious problems that could ruin the relationship.

Less stressful and more affordable holidays

Instead of spending money on luxurious vacations, exchanging gifts, and having parties, minimalist couples would rather spend time together and making it special without the need to spend a lot of money. As a minimalist, you will see how easy it is to find a fun activity to celebrate these special occasions rather than exchanging gifts. This helps couples make the most of their time with each other without denting their savings. After all, that essence of celebrating an occasion is to commemorate the love you're sharing. On top of that, the overall stress of the holiday season can be reduced as you don't have to worry about the perfect vacation or the perfect gift to give to each other.

Better health

Minimalism teaches the concept of "garbage in, garbage out," which you can also apply to your relationship. Since the beginning of my marriage, my wife and I have made a shift from eating healthy home cooked meals to eating out. Our health, as well as overall spending, has improved radically because of it.

Support for passions and values

In the first year of our marriage, my wife and I have decided to leave our higher paying jobs in order to follow our career paths and goals that we are striving for, because we thought our old jobs were giving us unnecessary stress that brings toxicity into our life. We believed that we needed to go for something that is much more aligned with our passions.

Now, this is not to say that minimalism can make your marriage perfect or fix any problem you could have. However, I really believe that any couples can benefit from following the basic values of minimalism.

Another main reason for failed marriage is expectations. Many couples, especially the newly married ones, expect too much of a fairytale romance story.

We have been so molded by today's society into thinking that you will get a "happily ever after" once you're married, that our expectations are extremely high and extremely far from reality.

There have been a lot of studies comparing arranged marriages and traditional marriages, and the results are not what you'd expect. According to studies, the level of "happiness" continuously soaring over the years for arranged marriages, and on the other hand, going down on the years for traditional marriages.

So, what might be the reason behind this? It is said that it was because arranged marriages began with low expectations, that's why they were pleasingly surprised and happy when things surpassed those initial expectations.

As research on satisfaction judgments shows, when expectations are low, these expectations are easier to meet making the arranged wedding couple more satisfied. While in a free-choice marriage, on the other hand, high expectations usually develop throughout a lengthy dating period. This puts couples up for failure after going through the honeymoon period.

Again, when you have minimalist expectations, you begin with zero and just add what is truly important. Important expectations might include "he/she knows how to listen to me", "he/she comforts me when I feel down", "he/she supports my dreams and goals." and they DON'T include "he/she doesn't give me enough compliments", "he/she doesn't earn enough money to buy a nice car", or "he/she always doesn't as productive as I want them to be."

4.2 Parenting

For many years, my family has been following a focused simplicity lifestyle. We know how complicated life can be, and we choose not to be taken over by this complication. That's why we choose to live with a minimalist lifestyle. And one of its major benefits that truly affect our family life is how it changes how we approach parenting.

So, in what ways, you may ask… Here are the ways minimalism affects parenthood…

It encourages you to take parenting seriously

It has become a habit for me to read reading materials about minimalist living. This regular dose of inspiration constantly reminds me to focus and make the most of every moment I spend with my loved ones, especially my kids. After all, they're not going to be little kids forever.

As parents, every time we weigh the different activities and desires of our lives, our families are our top priority. Having a family is a huge responsibility and we must take it very seriously.

It keeps you from spoiling your kids

For many parents, they think that being a good parent means giving everything they could to make their kids happy. But you have to remember that there is a fine line between what your kids need and what your kids want.

It's important to learn when to say "no" to things that you know they wouldn't need in the long term. Similarly, there's nothing wrong about giving your kids something they want from time to time.

For me personally, I give my kids treats as rewards after doing something they worked hard for. For example, I promised my 6-year-old kid to buy him his own computer if he gets straight A's in his class. This is in the hope to make him realize that if he really wants something, he has to work hard for it.

It helps you choose your battles wisely

No, I didn't mean a huge heated conflict, when I said "battle". I'm talking about the problems that we, as parents, make a big deal of sometimes. I'm talking about those small differences we may have with our kids that turn into disagreements.

As parents, we tend to think that we always know better than our kids – we think that we always know what's best for them. From the food they eat, clothes they wear, the friends they hang out with, to what clubs or sports to join at school and what career path to take, we usually have suggestions and sometimes, we tend to push those suggestions upon them.

Minimalism teaches us that while there are always unlimited options, the capacity is always limited. We need to choose where we spend our time and energy. In our effort to guide our kids' transition from being dependent to independent, we must learn to let go and let them make decisions for themselves.

When it comes to arguments – which something that is inevitable – minimalists acknowledge that there are times to stand our ground and there are times when it's just not worth it.

Keep in mind that if everything is a big deal, then there is no big deal

When dealing with arguments or making decisions that will affect the happiness of our kids, you have to think of what's at stake – their trust on you. These arguments can be considered as clutter and can be extremely distracting and might even cost us more than they are worth.

You become more fixated in what you teach your kids

While we want to raise our kids with the truth, you must not let that deceive you. You have to keep in mind that all truth is not similarly important.

It's possible to follow accurate details all my life and not find purpose and happiness. There will be things in life that are definitely important for my children to learn more than anything else. I always see to it that I focus my guidance on those things and help them to stand out amid all the information that comes their way as they grow up.

This is my question for you: If your kids are only to remember a thing or two about what you teach them while they are still under your wings, what do you want them to be?

Once you answer the question, emphasize those things in all that you say and do. There are surely other ways that minimalism can improve your parenting, but for me, the points mentioned above are what stand most significant.

For parents like me, you know that being a parent is one of the best roles in the world. And, as parents, we have to do everything we can to eliminate the clutter that will hamper us from our very important responsibility.

4.3 Career Life

Have you fallen into the idea that in order to be productive, you should work day in, day out?

If yes, then this scenario is probably familiar to you…

You get up very early; go to your work to start grinding. When it's already lunchtime, you stay in your chair, eat there, while carrying on working. As your coworkers start to leave at the end of the day, you stay late while you try in vain to finish all of your tasks and projects.

Few months passed, you are excited by the thought that you are progressing in getting the goal you are trying to achieve. But as time passes by, you're starting to realize that you are not really as productive as you initially thought, and you are struggling to sustain the chaotic pace.

If you choose to live like this, it shouldn't come as surprise when you get too burnt out by the end of the year.

So, what's the connection between productivity and minimalism?

The first thing you need to know is that there's a little-known (but certain) connection between productivity and minimalism.

Here is how you can look at minimalism in connection with productivity: *Delivering a task the simplest way possible.*

This might mean planning how you can manage your emails proficiently or knowing how to prioritize important tasks over the ones that can be done later. It might even mean generating the ability to focus fully on the laid-out task. The goal of minimalism is to get the tasks done easier… and more productive!

An example is when you have streamlined the way you make and present reports, you might find that you could do this task way faster than the time that it took you before. It just requires some time management and creativity to find for you to make the task as easier and simpler.

If you find yourself constantly not having enough time to do other tasks aside from your work, you must take a step back, and start looking for ways to make your workload easier for you to deal with. Every task that you make simpler can help save you a lot of time.

In spite of what you might have been taught at school, productivity and minimalism are essentially connected.

8 Ways Minimalism Can Boost Your Work Productivity

Now, let's take a look at some of the best ways to apply a minimalistic approach to your work.

- ✓ **Write a daily to-do list**

Start your working day (or any other day) by writing a to-do list. You can use a piece of paper or a smartphone app. It would only take a couple of minutes to create a list of all the things you'd like to do in the day ahead. And it is incredible how this simple activity could manifest your thoughts and help plan and carry out your day better.

- ✓ **Identify essential tasks**

When you have listed down all the tasks you need to put on your to-do list, scan through it. What are the ones you need to finish today? Can you identify them? In a lot of cases, the essential tasks should be finished first, and of course, listed down first. You can sort them out from the most important to the least important. Or some people like leaving exclamation mark (!) next to the item, so they can easily see identify the most critical ones.

- ✓ **Learn to focus and defeat distractions**

To be a successful minimalist, you must learn to develop laser focus. If you can't avoid distractions (such as loud conversations in an open-plan office), then by building powerful mental focus – distractions won't distract you anymore!

- ✓ **Turn tasks into daily habits**

Daily habits can be incredibly potent. They can break down complex tasks and turn them into bite-sized daily treats! For instance, you may work at a restaurant and need to clean the outside of the building every week. The cleaning might take you one hour to complete. Instead of this, you could build a daily routine of cleaning a part of the outside every day for 10 minutes. This will be easier and more enjoyable to complete than working a full hour on the task. It will also enable you to make it a habit – so you'll never have to motivate yourself to complete it.

✓ Stretch time

Stretching time is a skill that many people struggle with. But first, what does stretching time mean? Okay, so let's say that you are given two hours to create a slide show presentation. You begin the task, and if you are like many people, you will complete the tasks somewhere within the given two-hour mark. Now, imagine that rather than two hours, you were instructed to finish the task in one hour. Guess what – you can do it! This is what stretching time means. In order to save your time, try to assign yourself less time to finish your tasks.

✓ Be aware of the Pareto Principle

Have not heard of the Pareto Principle? No? But you probably know what 80/20 rule is, right? Well, they're the same thing! According to this principle, only 20% of our efforts will lead to 80% of our results. Now, look at it at the other way around… 80% of our efforts will lead to only 20% of our results! So, the trick here is to be fully aware of the 20% of actions that are generating most of the results. Be aware of these actions, concentrate on how you do them, and see how your productivity skyrockets.

✓ Take breaks on a regular basis

When you have a lot of things to do taking breaks from time to time is very tempting. But research has actually shown that those who are taking regular breaks from their work are actually more productive compared to those who don't. There are some science-backed reasons for getting regular breaks, which includes the fact that this is beneficial for maintaining our focus, help us remember important information and reevaluate our main goals. So, don't allow pressure to persuade you to keep working when you know to yourself that you need a break, which will trigger an instant boost to your productivity.

Begin adding these minimalist methods to your life right now. You will be surprised at how much productivity you'll get and more relaxed your mind would be by the end of the day.

4.4 Finances

We mentioned how minimalism can help us control finances on the earlier part of this chapter, but let's go a little bit deeper into this aspect of your life.

Again, minimalism can have a big positive effect on your finances in terms of saving money, getting out to debt, and building wealth. By applying a minimalistic approach can help you accomplish your financial goals easier and develop your attitude as you run through the process of building wealth. Let's talk about exactly how minimalism can help your finances below.

Minimalism can help you get clarity around your core values

As repeatedly mentioned above, minimalism has something to do with letting go of things that are not important in your life and focusing on things that really matter. The important things to you will normally play around your core values that when you identify, can help you with the process of eliminating things you don't need and embracing a more minimalistic approach to your life.

For example, if you love traveling, but you find yourself spending hours and hours on the internet browsing for items on sale to buy, which usually you don't really need, you can, instead, save that money to use on traveling, which something you know you really love.

On the other hands, if there are things that you really want to buy, try to not buy them right away. List them down and let a day or two to pass and ask yourself, "Do you I really need this item?" if you do, then go ahead and buy it, otherwise, just save your money for something else more important.

If you have not already, you can identify core values by asking yourself these two following question:

What are the experiences and things that really important to you?

Every time you look at your spending habits, does it align with your values?

Minimalism can mean buying fewer things, which of course, means spending less

A lot of people might not agree with this when it comes to this point as buying less doesn't necessarily mean spending less, but hear me out before rolling your eyes.

Most of the time, people purchase things because they're cheap and they think they're a great bargain. However, since they're very cheap, they're likely to end up purchasing more and more things they don't actually need and might even end up not liking. And rather than concentrating on their core values, it then becomes about focusing on how you can get a bargain rather than saving money.

So yes in a lot of instances, buying less means spending less which in turn means more money to pay off debt, to invest, and to save.

Minimalism allows you to focus on paying off your debt and saving

In keeping with the previous points, by buying less, you can have more money to spend on things that matter more to you, such as getting out of debt and saving money for your goals and for rainy days. It's going to be a win-win approach for minimalists – buying less means more clutter and potentially saving money

Minimalism brings contentment and peace of mind

Contentment and peace of mind are products of a minimalist's lifestyle. Having less clutter and avoiding compulsive buying can actually eradicate stress. And because you're just spending money on the things that really bring joy to your life, you'll have a great sense of satisfaction and happiness. You don't need to worry about keeping or maintaining or more importantly, paying for things you don't really need in the first place.

Deciding to take a minimalistic approach to life can be a major shift in lifestyle and is often a lengthy process. Even after several years, I continue to work on minimalism in my life, however, this approach to life is very fulfilling and totally worth it in my opinion.

Chapter 5

NEEDS & WANTS

Many are still confused with the difference between the things we need and the things we want. They crave for things they don't have and make themselves believe that they cannot simply live a good life without it, and often not satisfied until they lay their hands on what they want. When this mentality gets into a person to the extreme, it will usually cause destructive effects.

By letting this happen to us, we only have ourselves to blame. By putting our desires our first priority, things can be truly unpredictable. We are going to be required to live with our decisions and deal with them.

By living your life within your means does not necessarily mean you're always forgetting pleasure. It is simply about appreciating what life has already laid for you and accept the fact that having more doesn't always mean having it better.

Being in control over yourself can feel good, especially if it's something you have never done before. You will find that there are many other ways to feel satisfied without spending a lot of money and putting yourself in great debt. As cliché at it sounds... true happiness comes from the inside.

When you feel unhappy, chances are, that you have compared yourself to others, which leads to feeling inadequate. We tend to be jealous whenever we feel someone else is better at something that we want to be good at. However, when you stop comparing yourself to others, you will eventually get into the realization that your life could be truly fulfilling without always having what you want.

You don't have to fall victim to your urge to have everything you want. You can still be truly happy with what you already have. By searching from what's within you, we are able to find healthier ways to deal with your compulsions or anxiety.

So, you can take control if you really want to. Materials things should not have power over you and you can make a living simply with simple priority and high virtue.

Keep in mind that true happiness could simply be achieved once you start to accept yourself for what you are and forgive yourself for the mistakes you have committed. There's no need for you to make things complicated.

Knowing how to find the value in things you already have is a lesson anyone can take advantage of. If you cannot accept yourself, then don't expect to find true happiness and freedom from your insecurities.

5.1 What is the difference between things you need & things you want

There is an enormous difference between the words "need" and "want".

NEEDS

Obviously, these are the things that a person needs to stay alive. The things we need include food, water, shelter, clothing and not much else in this category, really. These are the things we need to stay alive.

In economics, need is basically referred to as something that is very necessary for a human being to survive. When a person fails to meet his needs, it would likely lead to the start of disease and limitation to a person's full functionality and efficiently in society, and even death.

There are two types of needs: physical needs and subjective needs. Physical needs are ones that are tangible things or things that can be measured. This category includes the food we eat, the water we drink, the shelter we live in, and the air we breathe. On the other hand, subjective needs are the ones that are usually seen to maintain the health of our mentality. Examples of these are love from others, self-esteem, and approval.

WANTS

A want is a thing a person desires, either in immediate time or later on in the future. Unlike the things we need, wants may differ from person to person. For example, you may want to have a new car, while another person wants to travel to another country.

Every person probably has his own list of things he wants, each with a different level of importance. Moreover, wants may also change throughout the period of time; unlike the things we need, which remain constant throughout our lifetime.

There is a fine line between these two and the gray area is when you badly desire to have a certain thing that it gets to the point that you're starting to think that it's something you need instead of want.

5.2 How To Identify the Thing You Need From Things You Want

It's easy to identify things that you need from the things you just want. Just ask yourself... Are you going to die without it? If yes, then it's a need. On the other hand, you will know if something is just something you want if you can literally live with it.

It's very obvious. We need shelter to live in. We need food to fill your stomach. Your neighbors would appreciate it if you looked at clothes to wear as a need. Your basic needs like these are non-negotiable, so you don't need to do get rid of them for the sake of minimalism and decluttering.

So, when do your basic needs turn into wants?

It is when you desire to have a bigger, grander house that is more than you need for your family, when you shop for too many food items that even usually expire before you consume them, when you buy a lot of clothes that you hardly ever wear.

When Wants Become Problematic

Of course, there is room to indulge in things we want, but as minimalist, you must only indulge in things that truly add value to your life. It's so easy to add clutter to your life these days, with the convenience online shopping offers, along with the constant discounts given away by different stores, and family and friends who like to give us gifts that we might not necessarily choose on our own. You will end up getting unnecessary possessions, occupying spaces that you could have had used for things that truly add value to your life.

Fortunately, when you see the difference between your real needs and wants, you can easily arrange your belongings in a more minimalist fashion, in the detached and rationalized way. By being committed to decluttering in this way, you can potentially find more calmness within yourself.

While the process doesn't offer an overnight result, it surely is worth it. It takes time to look through all our possessions, but it is well worth doing because the end result could be beneficial to all areas of your life.

5.3 How to Distinguish the Differences between the Two that Promote Minimalism

The straightforward answer to this question is very simple: The first step to minimalism lifestyle is to know the differences between these two. There are two major steps you need to do to get started in practicing this lifestyle.

Step 1: Spend at least a month or two getting rid of all the things you want. All of them – gone!

I know this is hard, but don't worry, once you're heading down the right path, and you have made all the necessary changes you need in your life, you are able to reintroduce your wants eventually, although, by the time that comes, you probably no longer want them anymore. Keep in mind that this is not to say that your wants are not important, in fact, they, in a way, add value to your life. However, they are not as important as the things we need.

Step 2: Once you've completely got rid of the things you want, the next thing for you to do is to reduce your needs by at least 50%. The more, the better.

Okay, you're probably thinking, *"But I need a place to live! I have to eat! I need my clothes, and I love them!"*

Okay, okay... you don't have to throw away everything: you don't have to move in a hut and eat just instant noodles. However, you can always significantly cut down your living expenses.

If you are renting, can you live in a smaller place to cut down your rent? Can you sell the gadgets you don't really need? Can you donate the clothes you haven't worn for a year or more? Can you lessen your expenses on food? Of course, you can!

While situations can be different from person to person, you can always reduce your expenses and live a lot more deliberately. This is the high price of pursuing a minimalist lifestyle. Unfortunately, a lot of people are not willing to pay the price. But then again, it is human nature for us to always want more. Especially today where consumerism blocks us from knowing how much is enough and too much.

But when you successfully detach yourself from the clutches of material things, you will worry less; and when you get rid of your worries, you can easily focus on more important things that give you happiness and satisfaction.

It doesn't mean you must go now and start throwing away every single thing you have, it's necessary for you to plan accordingly, and once you are ready, the right decision can easily be recognized.

All beautiful changes take time and need the right action taking. Changes are definitely scary, but they can really be necessary. And even though big changes usually take a simple move, they are not easy, but you know what they say: nothing worth doing is ever easy.

Chapter 6

Optimizing Life for Minimalism

In this chapter, we're going to talk about the step-by-step ways of becoming minimalist through the principles of decluttering.

I tried to find the exact definition of "declutter" and I definitely cannot find the results in any dictionary of English vocabulary. However, it's a word widely used by many people today.

I assume, though, it is a synonym for the word unclutter. According to Free Dictionary Online, declutter referred as "to simplify and/or eliminate mess, disorder, obstacles, etc."

On the other hand, the definition for the word, "clutter" can be easily found. In fact, it is found in any dictionary and it is defined as "a collection of things lying about in an untidy mass".

So, it just means that declutter is the antonym of clutter. It implies to arrange things, to put items in a place where they should be.

Now, let's look at the meaning of the word, "organize." This word implies, "to arrange into a structured whole; order".

So, every time we organize, we are putting them in the right order/place (decluttering) in a structure having an efficient and useful solution to keep those items (organizing).

Another term which complements the word declutter is the word "clean". It seems like every time you declutter a space, it gets cleaner; however, it doesn't always mean that the area is cleaned.

Clean, as you probably know, is actually the process of eliminating stain, dirt, dust, etc. Decluttering and cleaning go hand-in-hand -- you cannot perform one properly without the other.

Another word we usually hear when declutter is the center of the topic is the word "hoarding" – but what does it mean? In most dictionaries you'll find, hoarding would be referred to as "to amass and hide or store away; reserve in the mind for future use".

There are certainly different levels of hoarding. However, in general for this term, a hoarder is someone who is serious in collecting clutter thinking that those items are valuable and have great use in the future. This is the problem though, for people who are serious hoarders, everything has value to them. This results in the accumulation of things that sometimes can be out of control.

Now... how do these terms relate to minimalism? These are the keywords you initially need to understand to attain the real essence of minimalism and to learn how you can successfully apply it in every aspect of your life.

Now that you know the differences of these words, let's go ahead and talk about the ways in becoming a minimalist through the principle of decluttering.

6.1 A Simple Plan for Home Declutter

Having a good plan is one of the most essential steps of decluttering a home.

The reason behind this is generally psychological: By having a clear plan for attaining a goal, will give you more motivation. First of all, it helps you to have "the end in sight" and secondly, will give you easy-to-follow instructions, which is a lot easier than debating and thinking to yourself, "how should I clean the fridge today?" for example.

So, here's a simple plan to use on the mission of getting your home decluttered easily. By following your plans accordingly in a religious manner, you can easily complete the task in just a week, by putting in at least an hour a day. Sounds easy, right? Because it is.

First, you have to decide on the steps that you are going to implement for the task.

The following are the most important steps:

(Note: You can add or modify this list according to your preference or situation)

Step 1: Gather all the things that "bother" you and you no longer use.

Step 2: Categorize them into two groups - one group for the things you want to throw out and one group for the things you want to give away or donate.

Step 3: Have enough space for the things you don't want to throw away.

Step 4: Organize them into a storage space.

Easy, right? These are the basic steps for decluttering your house, and even if you only choose to follow these simple steps, you will already see a great improvement.

As you can probably notice, I did not divide the tasks by rooms/areas at home. This is because I believe that it could be quite frustrating to have a vague task like "declutter the living room". This could just lead to a low level of productivity

There should be specific tasks/steps to perform decluttering to each part of the house.

But going back to the point where I mentioned "things that bother you", you're probably wondering what this means exactly?

Okay, so look, the main objective of home declutter is to minimize the stress brought by clutter and to make your home a place where you can relax and feel good both mentally and physically.

So, if your kitchen, or even your bedroom is pretty cluttered, but it does not bother you and does not make you think that you need to do something about it, you can leave it alone for the meantime. You must focus first on the parts of the house that bothers you the most - the most problematic parts.

Once you find the parts of the house you want to take care of first, the next step is to estimate how much time every step would probably take. The estimation will depend on how busy you are and how big the area is. If doing the first step will require more or less an hour, setting it for one day will be enough. On the other hand, if it takes more than that, perhaps setting 2 days is good enough.

Generally, only the fourth step should take the longest and you can divide it into 3 to 4 days.

6.2 Decluttering Your Home

Home should be the most comfortable, safest place for us. But in order for it to bring us the relaxation we need and for it to nurture a positive effect, it has to be clean and well-organized. But by having piles of unwanted items all around the home, it can certainly hamper your chance to maximize the purpose of your home.

The main idea of living minimalistic sounds attractive to a lot of people. Many also aspire to do it, but it seems like it's easier said than done. But that's pretty understandable. But when you know how to do it right, you'll be on your way to a successfully minimalistic home. Here are some tips you can follow for decluttering any part of your house.

Pick the Right Time When You Want to Start Decluttering

Don't start the process in one room when you know you won't have enough time to do every inch of the room. Maybe, it's best to pick a time when someone else can give you a hand.

For example, if you have one hour to spare to do some decluttering, and you know that decluttering the garage is not going to be realistic to be done in that sort of timeframe, you can move to another place in the house that would be more ideal. Perhaps the kitchen or the bathroom?

That is enough time to go through the cupboards or drawers and throw away the junk you no longer need. Doing so would be a great accomplishment.

Divide Your Home into Different Sections

As I keep mentioned earlier, don't do the entire home at once. Decluttering your home, especially if you're the only one to do it, is best done by taking one room at a time.

When you choose to declutter one cabinet in the kitchen, one cabinet in the bathroom, and all the cabinets in your closet at the same time, you will often find you will just lose steam quickly.

Whenever you have to declutter, you can always keep going back to that one room you're working on and throw more and more things until you are satisfied. This may sound like a lot of work, but finishing even just a room is super rewarding.

It's really important to make sure that you really focus while you're decluttering. Remove all the items out of that cabinet and go through each of them.

Make Three Separate Piles

- The Keep Pile
- The Toss Pile
- The Donate Pile

When you're done putting the items on the right pile, dispose of the toss pile right away. Carry the donate pile and place it in the car. The next time you have to go with your car, you can drop off the pile at your local donation center.

So, what would this look like for each room? Let's talk about each room in the house.

- ❖ **Bedrooms**

As you browse around your master bedroom, do you see things that are not in the right places? Or things you no longer use and that could be moved to a better place, given away, or even thrown out? Below are some ideas you may want to consider:

- ❖ Is there a pile of magazines or books on top of the nightstand that you are planning to read, but can't find time to read?
- ❖ Are there accessories and jewelry that are unorganized or no longer used?
- ❖ Are there too many framed pictures all over the place?
- ❖ Is there rubbish under the bed?

When you start looking around, you will probably see a lot of things that need throwing out or moving into their proper place.

After clearing all the tabletop areas, now you have to start going through the shelves, drawers, and storage areas you have. Keep in mind that if you don't use it, it's probably better for it to go.

If you find clothes you no longer use, donate them. Some of the things you can donate also include shoes, bed sheets, blanket, and even curtains. Our goal is to minimize our stuff as much as possible. If you don't use it, there's no point of keeping it.

Now, it's time to do some cleaning. You've moved and organized a lot of items in your room. You've probably also noticed several areas that are filthy and dusty.

Clean and polish all the furniture. Decluttering involves cleaning and removing dust and dirt.

Now, let's look into what you want to keep and get the organization started. Perhaps, you can group items in your armoire better to keep them more organized and easier to find when you need them.

For things that you use on regular basis, place them where you can easily get them. No one wants to spend hours looking for keys in the morning.

Look around and see if you have to move anything else make any other changes to make the bedroom perfect.

- ❖ **Kid's Room**

Over the past couple of days, my wife and I have been working on decluttering the room of our toddlers. It is not easy. This is especially challenging because sometimes, they just can't help themselves but clutter even while you are cleaning. So, here is what we do to declutter them...

The toys are the first things I go through. And I get pretty ruthless when it comes to decluttering toys. All ill see is toys that are broken, have missing pieces or the ones I haven't seen played with for months so all are heading to the trash. It's unfortunate that many toys get put in a toss pile, but I still try to find ones that are ideal for donation.

Before organizing the kids closet, I go through their toys first. Of course, I first organize the ones that we are going to keep. The bigger toys go into the storage box we keep under the bed when not in use, while the smaller ones are on the shelves and smaller bins.

After organizing the toys, I go straight to the clothes. I do the same process once again, but this time, of course, with the clothes. The first time we decluttered, we had to let go of a lot of clothes. We sorted through the clothes and categorized them. Offseason clothes and clothes that would be passed down to the younger kids went into its specific box, while the others were prepared for donation.

You can repeat the same process for any room in your house. Declutter and organize one room and then move on to the next until the whole room is done.

❖ Kitchen

Having an organized workplace is going to help you to be efficient and effective in whatever you do. The same thing applies when you're working in a kitchen. If your things are placed all over the place, you might end up wasting a lot of your time looking for those kitchen utensils you need to prepare your meals. On the other hand, by having an organized and clean kitchen, your life is going to be a lot easier and you'll have a smoother cooking experience.

Here are some ways to organize the kitchen and declutter your kitchen area.

1. Rearrange your kitchen stuff. You can start with the drawers because they're very easy to organize and declutter. Think of the stuff in your kitchen that you'll be keeping or throwing away. What do you use regular, and what do you rarely use?

2. After organizing, start cleaning your kitchen item storage. Wipe and wash them down in order to remove dust and other unwanted particles in your utensils.

3. Put back all your kitchen tools after cleaning the storage. Yet, you need to consider the flow of your movements within the kitchen. Think of how you prepare and cook your food. By doing this, you'll have an idea where you can place the important kitchen tools and those that are hardly used. Put all your pans and pots organized properly and your spices and condiments in the pantry.

4. Have just enough storage boxes. If you think you don't have enough storage space, then maybe you should try and make some. By doing this, your kitchen items are only going to be contained in one place. You could also use a separator so you can easily differentiate the knives from your other cutleries.

Furthermore, big appliances that are in your kitchen such as the refrigerator must be far from the door. This is an important thing to consider when you are looking to organize all your things.

In order to organize the kitchen and declutter kitchen things can be very easy regardless of how big the kitchen is. You should try and think what will make you more effective and efficient in your chores.

- ❖ **Bathroom**

Decluttering your bathroom can be one of the bigger challenges to organizing. While it's usually the smallest part of the house, we can usually find a lot of things in it. Fortunately, there are a lot of easy organizing techniques and products that can help you keep your bathroom looking decluttered and organized.

With a little creativity, you can successfully declutter your bathroom in no time.

Take stuff out of your bathroom, what are the things that you really need and don't need. Carry a garbage bag along with cleaning supplies

Go through those drawers. Throw out the old makeup if it's not being used anymore! You can move those items you store on top into a drawer. Your bathroom is going to be less cluttered. Using drawer organizers helps keep your bathroom drawers in order and don't forget to put those items you frequently use on top.

Is your body wash, shampoo, and conditioner sitting on the floor of your shower or on the handrail of the door? Has your shower floor turned into a blend of bottles? Are you tired of bending down to pick up what you need? You can also find different kinds of affordable and stylish shower caddies available today that will not only declutter and organize your shower but will also add aesthetics to your bathroom.

You can literally make the cabinets in your bathroom an organized storage area, neat and decluttered. First of all, you need to organize and purge! Get rid of that old shampoo that you bought and did not like. The same goes for anything that you have not used. I know that a lot of the time we buy things that we don't like but hate the idea of throwing them away. Now is the time to throw it away and organize your bathroom cabinets.

General Guidelines

- ❖ Check the drugs/medications that are past the expiration dates, throw out the expired ones.
- ❖ Establish a ruthless mindset
- ❖ Establish another storage area for rarely used items so they don't clutter your bathroom but are still easily reached
- ❖ Keep massively sized products bought at warehouse stores elsewhere
- ❖ Makeup also expires!
- ❖ Put an old sheet or beach blanket on the floor to use as a temporary staging area.
- ❖ Use your storage space only for items you are still using and use regularly

- ❖ **Living Room**

A lot of people are reluctant to consider organizing their living room. They think that because the living room is for living in, it's natural for this part of this house to accumulate clutter. But this shouldn't be different from other parts of the house when it comes to decluttering – a better living room is better to live in.

First of all, consider every activity that takes place in the living room and then decide if those activities are best done in this part of the house. Is it the best place to teach your kids their assignment? If you would rather make a comfy corner for your kids to study, then do that. Otherwise, consider defining a special corner for your kids when you need to help them study.

Try to work systematically, one category at a time, pull all things out of each space and group items as one. Make decisions on what you are going to do with those items based on the answer to the questions, "When was the last time I used this?" "Does it serve its purpose?" "Can't I live without it?"

Always be honest with yourself and cut back your items; if you are being honest, it is going to be easier to make decisions. Have specific boxes that you can label 'charity', 'sale', and 'keep'. If you have not decluttered this area for a long time, remember that what you loved and used before, might be something that you no longer need now. When you have decluttered every category and put everything on where they should be, moving around the living room would be a lot easier and more comfortable.

Top tips for decluttering the living room

- Take your time to evaluate what is working and what is not working in the space.
- Only keep items that you love and currently use.
- Ask family members whether or not they want to keep the items.
- Use the chance to clean as you go.

❖ Garage

Believe it or not, most people choose to leave their vehicles out on the driveway all the time. Normally, this happens because there is no room left in the garage to actually park their car, as they are just rammed with junk. If you are having the same dilemma, you may not want to miss this one.

You can start your garage decluttering process by looking through every item in the garage, one by one. Consider how long the item has been stored in the garage. If it's something you haven't used for more than three years, then maybe it's time for it to go.

One of the most common items people seem to love keeping are cans of paint. This is something that just has to go. It's possible as well that they are partly dried up already anyway.

There are a lot of things that make their way into the garage. Sports equipment is another culprit that gets 'permanently' stuck in the garage. Stop keeping any sporting items that are already broken. It's not a good idea to play tennis using a broken racket.

Of course, auto parts are always found in the garage. If you no longer have the vehicle that the parts belong to, it's time for you to throw them away. And of course, if they are broken just dispose of them right away. The next thing to evaluate is ladders. Unless they are in good condition, safe, and sturdy enough to be used, there shouldn't be a place for them in your garage.

Go through everything and even evaluate your tools. Think about how often you use each item, dispose of any items that you never use. If it's broken and cannot be fixed then, of course, throw it away.

Organize What's Left

When you're already done and all of the clutter is out, it is time to start organizing. First, see how much space your vehicles will take up and then use what's left by placing items in the spaces based on their types and uses:

Regularly Used: Keep items that you use on regular basis. This includes rugs, shopping bags, and pet leashes within easy reach – maybe on hooks by the door.

Bigger Items: Use the two back corners of the garage to keep bulkier items like a lawn mower or snow thrower.

Hardly Used: Place items you rarely use like seasonal decorations or snow tires, on higher shelves of sturdy shelving units or you may want to consider installing a ceiling storage system. Just see to it that these new storages are not blocking the door.

Tools and Bicycles: Tools like rakes and shovels and bicycles are best stored by hanging on the wall.

Note: If you are using cardboard boxes as your storage containers, you might want to consider investing in some plastic bins that are going to keep insects, molds, and rats from taking up residence in your house.

Keep It Tidy

When you're finally done with everything, you will have a cleaner garage that's organized nicely. The next step is to make efforts in maintaining your garage in that state by doing the following.

- ✓ Keep floor space as free as possible.
- ✓ Spray for pests every now and then to keep insects at bay.
- ✓ Sweep and scrub down the floors on a regular basis to remove dirt.
- ✓ And the most important step of all: Repeat the process at least every two months.

KEEP ONLY THE THINGS YOU ABSOLUTELY LOVE.

There is no point in keeping things just because. Really, keep only the things that you really love! I think there's nothing wrong with keeping an item that reminds you of your childhood – but don't keep all of them!

I know this is something that is difficult for many people. It can be difficult for some to give up the sweater their grandma gave them when they were little or for parents, their kids' clothes. But always remember that those are only material things and memories are forever and something can be built over and over again.

You might have items you don't really want to keep around, but you still actually need to keep. For example, certain cleaning supplies. In this case, I'd suggest only keeping just one of each needed item. Having something like 5 different window cleaners is just not necessary. Also try to pare down cleaning rags and other smaller miscellaneous items. Keep it simple!

Now that you've organized your space, maintaining it should be the next thing you need to worry about. You probably don't want to hear this, but decluttering is a process. Especially if you are decluttering a house.

The good thing is, once you have totally decluttered your house, maintaining it will not be as difficult.

As more or new things come into your house, take out the stuff you have no longer value for. Always think of the reasons why you wanted to live a simpler life and declutter, to begin with. Don't go back to how it was even before you get started.

Creating a housekeeping routine is an effective way of maintaining your home. My wife and I switch morning routines that keep our home clean and decluttered.

6.3 Decluttering Your Material Possessions

Are You Possessed by Your Possessions?

This is the first question you must answer if you are thinking about decluttering. So, what can you do for your possessions to possess you?

Now that I discovered the benefits of decluttering, clutter has become something that truly gets to my nerves. You can call me a neat freak.

After letting go of most of my possessions, I immediately reap the benefits it offered to me and my family. On top of the mental benefit it offers, I also enjoy the fact that I can now easily locate everything I needed.

Throughout the process of decluttering our home from possessions that don't add value to our lives, there are several things I and my family learned...

1. It helps in letting go of the past to make more room for the future

The whole decluttering experience will make you realize that that most of the things you are holding on to have already served their purpose in your life and at some point, you have to let go. It's very difficult to move ahead in life if you keep clinging to the past. Letting go of the sentimental items can be very hard. Seeing the old greeting cards, photos, and mementos lets you close chapters of your life that ended but you still keep holding on to.

It helps you free up mental energy for future undertakings and relationships. One of the most important things you'll realize throughout the process is that all items you dispose of or donate to charity already served their purpose. They might have given you a lot of joy or taught you a great lesson. By understanding this, you are freeing your mind for future experiences and development.

2. It teaches you to be grateful for what you already have

Again, there's nothing wrong with material things and in fact, I still have a lot of things that I find hard to let go of. However, I never let them become a priority to the point that they drag me off my track. For me, throwing away material possessions that are not being used, help free your mind from unimportant things and help you focus on things that are truly important, this on top of helping you grow as a person, improving your relationships, and helping others along the way. By surrounding yourself with only things you love, it helps you realize that there's no point of going nuts over a new gadget or garment. And more importantly, it helps you see the concept of quality over quantity.

3. It improves your sense of focus

When there is a pile of rubbish on my desk, I always find myself struggling to finish things I'm working on. But the moment I clear up my desk and put everything in their right places, working becomes easier. From a neurological standpoint, this completely makes a lot of sense.

Whether it is your office desk or bedroom, the mess in your surroundings can lead to a negative effect on your capability to focus and process the train of thoughts. That is exactly what neuroscientists at Princeton University discovered when they looked at task performance individuals in an organized versus disorganized environment. The final conclusion of the study showed that the physical clutter you have in your surroundings contends your attention, these results in lower levels of performance and higher levels of stress. Clutter essentially triggers the brain to multitask. So, getting rid of it will help transform you into a concentrating machine.

Effective Ways to Get Rid Of Unnecessary Possessions

❖ Tear down the museum

I used to be fearless in my youth. I made a lot of friendships and made a history for myself that seemed worth to remember. So, I held on to all the trinkets from my past. Going forward to the future, I was rewarded with a lot of items that I did not have any room for in the present. I wanted to invite people over the house and even throw a party, but I couldn't even figure out where to put them all. So, what I did was, I took pictures of the items that were important to me, but I was still ready to let go. They are always going to be parts of my past, but they can't be with me, physically, forever.

❖ Evaluate real value

Most of the items I owned that have value to me were computer equipment. Every time I looked at it all, I would just see dollar signs. But then, looking at their economic perception, it was just a delusion. I was giving importance to those old computers based on the money I spent on them instead of their current market value: almost nothing. During decluttering, I sold many of my used electronics and sold them for $70.

❖ Not everything is worth the fix

Most of the broken things that piled up in my garage are gym shoes. I didn't throw them away because I was convinced that I will be able to get them fixed eventually. My wife held the shoes up in front of me, one by one, and asked a couple of questions: "If you saw a pair of these shoes in a store today, do you think you're going to buy them?" and "How much are you willing to pay for them if you're willing to buy them?" I admitted that I wouldn't buy those shoes again.

❖ Inform your loved ones

I'm a part of a minimalist group on Facebook, where minimalist people share their minimalist lifestyle-related thoughts and questions. One of the "dilemmas" members are experiencing is the number of gifts they get on special occasions. You see, this is something that shouldn't be a problem for many, in fact, it's a good thing. But for someone who tries to live in a minimalist lifestyle, this is something that can be a trigger for them for accumulating more and more stuff again. The solution to this is simple. Let them know about your lifestyle and tell them what you'd rather get. This could be a specific item that you like or even money.

❖ Just admit that you don't like it

As I organized my stuff, I slowly become aware of the fact that I did not even want to keep it all. There were things that I didn't really like but I didn't particularly hate either – and kept with them out of pure apathy. These are the easiest things to let go. It has only taken me a little motivation to pack up a couple of boxes and give them away to those who need them more.

❖ Know what you really need

Usually, what we need is just related to the thing we have. For example, I had an oven toaster, but I decided to let it go because I had a small toaster that is enough to toast my loaves. I also loved reading and my books were dear to me, but I made a decision of rehoming them.

❖ Let go of the guilt

When my grandpa passed away, I inherited his collection of 30 rusty knives, 5 toolboxes, and a copper watch he loved to wear. For many years, I kept them all. Eventually, I realized that if my grandpa was alive, he would probably replace the knives and the toolboxes. I disposed of them, but I kept the watch and still wear it from time to time.

❖ **Accept that "one day" may not even come**

Most people hoard stuff because they think that a time will come they will have to use them. My wife kept the wedding dress she wore 7 years ago. She didn't want to throw it away. But it was just taking too much room in our closet. Also, unless we are planning to remarry or wait for our 5-year-old daughter to get married and inherit it, no one is really going to use it.

6.4 Decluttering your Gadgets

There is no denying that technology can truly make life easier and more entertaining. It also helps us connect with our loved ones from anywhere in the world at any time. But between necessities such as computers, smartphones, cameras, as well as old favorites such as the CD or cassette tapes collection, you have collected throughout the decades, you surely have a big a pile of clutter from this.

You might feel a little overwhelmed just thinking about organizing everything from chargers to cables to cassette tapes to computer accessories. However, when you do it, you will enjoy how your home becomes a much safer and more comfortable place, and you no longer need to waste time looking for misplaced headphones and memory cards.

Why It's Important to Organize Your Tech

First of all, it can help you realize why you are actually doing the process of decluttering in the first place. Safety is one of the main reasons; neglected cables can be a fire hazard, and cords or gadgets left underfoot can lead to tripping. Another reason is cleanliness; it's harder to vacuum, dust, or wipe down a cluttered area, so getting rid of that barrier makes cleaning a lot easier and so much more likely to get done.

Another motivator is aesthetics, of course. Large unused appliances, ugly wires, and remote controls lying all over the place can make even a well-organized room look untidy.

Lastly, technology must make your life easier, not more difficult. If searching for the right charger or adapter, or just plain use of any of your devices gives you stress, that is all the more reason for you to declutter.

Tech Clutter Hotspots

Every home has particular areas that are easily overtaken by technology and its associated clutter. And while these hotspots will vary from household to household, the most common clutter culprits are the following.

Around Outlets

There is always a place where all the cables snake along the floor — or for wall-mounted TVs, skid down the wall. Some of the most effective ways to deal with this include hooks and clips that stick to your desk or walls, clamping cords down in better order; slim tubes that suit over cords and can be set up to the wall or floor then painted over, almost blending the cables into the wall; and boxes that fit over power strips, concealing the unappealing gathering of plugs. A lot of big hardware stores and websites offer an apparently endless collection of products to help organize cables and cords. By searching for "cord/cable organizer" online, you will have a lot of products to choose from and definitely find the one that is perfect for your needs.

Home Offices or Other Designated Work Areas

Computers, printers, and other office supplies are usually found here. And because it's a place where you spend endless hours to work, you will want to make sure that it is a comfortable place. In order to clean up your workspace, the first thing you need to do is to get rid of any tech you no longer use, such as old laptops and broken spare parts. After that, you must determine how often you use all the things that are left. The things that you use all the time, such as the laptop can always be left on your desk but try to move the ones you rarely use like the scanner maybe. Put them on a shelf and just get them down when needed. When you need to upgrade or replace an old device, you may want to choose devices that perform multiple tasks. For example, instead of buying different devices for printing, scanning, photocopying, find a single device that is capable of doing all these three things.

Entertainment Areas

These are usually found in the living room and bedroom areas. In order to clean up these areas, you can focus on clearing surfaces by baskets or boxes where you can put all your small tech stuff when you're not using them. Once putting back the remotes to the basket has become a habit, they will no longer clutter up the place. This means no more fishing for the remote under in the sides of the couch!

That Spot near The Door Where Items Usually Accumulate

This could be a kitchen counter, console table, or the first piece of furniture you see as soon as you enter the door, where you leave your phone, together with your keys and glasses. You don't have to fight the urge and convenience of putting your things here but adapt with your habits and the layout of the space and out a tray or basket in this clutter zone. This will help you keep small items from cluttering up the area and also prevent them from strangely wandering off.

Organizing Your Collections

The abundance of new technology — mixed with ever-growing shopping opportunities —makes it easier than ever to accrue gadgets, whether your weakness is for new camera lenses or audio equipment. And even though music lives in the cloud today, and watching movies can be done online, many people still don't want to give up their records, DVDs, VHS tapes, cassette tapes, and other collections you have built around earlier times of technology.

Collections have made a lot of people happy — but that changes when you already have to organize them. As with any decluttering project, the first step is to be truly honest with yourself and of course, get rid of the ones you no longer use. You can bring old CDs to a state or local government recycling center, if that's available in your area, or send them by mail to an organization such as the CD Recycling Center of America. You may also want to send them along with the CDs of old installation software and user manuals you have no use for anymore.

Next, manage the items that you hardly use, like old home movies you haven't watched in decades but impossible to let go. You can store these collections out of sight and out of your way in a basement, or storage unit. Pick containers that can protect your items from mold and water damage, pack them properly, and put a clear label on them. You must be aware that extreme changes in humidity or temperature can damage electronic gadgets.

Now it's time to arrange everything you want to keep easily accessible. The easiest storage options are attractive boxes or open shelving. Measure the size of your collection carefully before you buy any new storage accessories or furniture; Take a bookshelf that is too big or a cabinet that is too small and not just will you have tech clutter, but furniture clutter too.

If you're thinking about where to put your collection, choose the general organizing guidelines of keeping items close to where they will be used, which means, remote controls should be closed to TV and audio system.

Sorting Out the Small Things

A great deal of tech clutter is due to the accumulation of small add-ons and accessories: power strips and cables, headphones and thumb drives, chargers and batteries, memory cards, as well as their little plastic sleeves, those small foam earbud covers, and so forth.

The moment you have removed anything you know you will never need again, the easiest way to arrange small tech items that will keep them all in a proper place: a cupboard, a shelf, a box, or anything as long as it works in your home. By doing that, you would not have to race from the hall closet to the office to the basement whenever you need to use an extension cord or an SD card.

However, a different method may work better for your specific situations. For example, if you always travel, you may want to keep travel-related gadgets items – such as external chargers and adapters – in a small pouch in your luggage. Or, you might want to keep the technology you use for work or a specific hobby in the rooms where you only use them and keep other household tech items in a different place.

As a rule of thumb, you should work with your own lifestyle and personal preferences. If you always instinctively check your kitchen drawer every time you need extra batteries, then put them there. If your house has an area that is specifically good for storage, make good use of it. When you declutter and organize, keeping it up should feel easy and natural. If you're having trouble, you are probably trying to defy your instincts or the arrangement of your space.

And again, labeling everything is a game changer; this could save you a lot of time whenever you have to identify which cable goes with which phone and other devices. You can use a label maker for an even look, or just get tape and a marker. Using colored tape is always a good idea to identify amongst a sea of black and white cords. In order to keep cords from getting untidy, wind them all and secure it using a bread wire tie, cable tie, rubber band, or Velcro strip before putting it back to the drawer or box.

Getting Rid of Unwanted Tech

If you have a stack of unused laptops, cameras, phones, and other various gadgets anywhere in your home, you're not the only one. If you are holding on to them for a reason that you are no sure of, ask the product manufacturer or your local government in order to see if they have a recycling program. A lot of companies like Staples, Best Buy, and Apple offer electronics recycling services. You can also donate old computers and other items to charitable organizations, or make some money by donating them.

A lot of electronics are made with hazardous materials and shouldn't be just thrown in the trash; your city or county must give instructions on how to safely throw away these items in your area. And ensure that your personal information is removed and all hard drives are properly backed up, and carefully overwritten or erased.

As mentioned already, you are able to recycle CDs of the installation software and user manuals you don't have a use for anymore. You could probably declutter your paper user manuals as well; see to it that the information is found online, and then recycle all those little booklets and empty some space in your household files.

Decluttering is part of life, and like technology, it can inspire you to keep going and organizing additional parts of your home.

Technology is continually evolving, which means a lot of households are always acquiring new gadgets as older devices become out-dated.

While we are usually desperate to own the latest gadgets in the market, we are less eager to clear out what we currently have. This mainly boils down to not having an idea on what to do with old smartphones, laptops, audio players, and so on. On top of that, worry over getting rid of something that is important – a cord we are abruptly going to need, for instance, or confidential data.

However, nobody has space for old devices and cords to be piling up in their homes; so, here are some effective tips to declutter your gadgets:

6. 5 Decluttering Your Schedule

Reducing the number of your possessions is essential to embracing a minimalism lifestyle. However, what is equally important is decluttering your schedule and limiting what you put on your calendar.

With today's technology, housework, job meetings, meal prep, and dealing with family needs has become much more efficient. Technology surely has the capability to save us a lot of time. But why is that it seems like we are much busier than those who lived decades ago?

The reason for this is partly because it is something we want.

Today, having a busy schedule has become the main indicator of high status. We boast about how full our calendar is and how many individuals are competing for our time. We tend to think that this shows how important we are.

We live busy lives – may it be by choice or circumstance. Nonetheless, it's a reality of the world we live in today.

Because of this, there are a lot of people who are hoping to minimize their schedule but cannot seem to find the margin to do so. In this part of the book we are going to look into this further.

But first of all, how is decluttering your schedule beneficial? While decluttering a schedule is obviously a great way to repel the temptation of procrastination, there are other ways it benefits a person in a way that it supports the minimalism lifestyle.

❖ Create More Free Time

This may sound a bit backward because a lot of people think they are procrastinating when they choose to do nothing instead of spending their time working. However, if you come to think of it, it's only considered procrastinating if you have got assignments to do but choose not to do them. By decluttering your schedule, you will be able to make time in your day when you can just relax and do anything you want – you will know how to get things done by a specified time. By doing this, you will not be able to waste your free time worrying about what you must be doing for the time being.

❖ You Know When You're Being Unproductive

Sometimes, it's not easy to acknowledge whether we are using our time wisely or not. For example, those who work online don't have bosses to tell them what to do or watch over you if you are doing your work right. If you have to follow a schedule and follow it, you will know what to do and what you should avoid. If you cannot finish things within a schedule, you can pinpoint what distracted you and so you can eliminate this next time around.

❖ You Can Have Peace Of Mind

Do you constantly say, "There are not enough hours in the day"? You may think you have lots of things to do but not have enough time to get them all done. But by decluttering your schedule, you will have the peace of mind knowing that your tasks will get done without needing to lose sleep and forgetting to do other things.

❖ You Can Set Your Goals Accordingly

One of the best things about schedules is that they can also be used as you goals. It's not hard to be thrown off-course in terms of achieving something. You can assign time to tasks that are going to help you to attain a long-term goal, such as being able to lift 300 lbs weight at the gym by the end of the year, as well as short-term goals, like finishing work's assignment by the end of the day.

❖ Learn How to Set a Deadline

When you are working on one thing, it's so easy to forget other tasks that are equally important. No one wants to pull all-nighters studying and working only to remember that you forgot to finish something that is due the next day. You are can highlight your deadlines on your schedule in order for you to have a clear vision of how much you have to accomplish before they arrive. Then, you can make a decision whether to do your projects all at the same time, or for a short period of time.

❖ You Don't Double-Book

So, someone asked you to go out on a Friday night, and you agreed. But then you realize too that you have got something else important to do at that time. You don't want that person to drive all the way to meet you while you ditch the plan, however, you can't also ditch that important thing you need to do. You can avoid disasters like this by always being aware of what you need to do and when.

❖ Being More Productive

There is nothing that improves productivity better than a schedule. When you are looking at all the things you have to accomplish in the following days, weeks, months, or years, you are bound to be more efficient as you know you don't want to be stuck with everything last minute. You can jump from task-to-task rather than thinking you have more free time than you actually have. In the end, you will probably see that you have accomplished a lot so that you can now relax have more time to relax.

Now that you know the benefits of decluttering your schedule, how can you experience these benefits? Here are effective ways to declutter your busy schedule.

1. Wake Up Early or Stay Up Late

In a perfect world, you can choose whenever you want to be productive. Sit down on your desk, start working while waiting for the day to end. Unfortunately, being productive is not as simple as just plugging in for humans—we experience a kind of energy and creativity at a certain period of the day.

So, when is the right time for you to work? Some of us are naturally born as either an early bird or a night owl. According to research, we cannot choose to be a night owl or a morning bird, because our biological clock, or chronotype, is mostly genetic.

Now, only about 15% of us are real early birds, and 20% are natural night owls, while the rest of us are in-between. Now, you're the only one to decide what you truly are. Find out what you are and choose what time of the day, or night, you are more productive and then set your schedule depending based on when you are productive.

2. Turn off The Television/Wi-Fi

According to statistics regarding our screen time, we spend an average of about 10 hours a day in front of the TV or computer. Aim to reclaim your control over your life and home by reducing your time in front of your electronics. Ideally, you may want to spend only 45 minutes a day. I know this could be a drastic change for many, but don't worry because this does not have to be a permanent change if you find it difficult, but it wouldn't hurt to try. So, for a period of time, it is able to give you the extra time you need to declutter your home during a busy schedule.

3. Clarify Your Priorities

Clarifying your priorities is another important step to decluttering your schedule. To me, my priorities include my family, job, time with nature, spare time for reading, going out, etc. Every time I look at my schedule, it was full of tasks like happy hour, social events, and weekends are full of housework. When I decided to make a change, I stopped committing to most of those events and suddenly, I had free time to do constructive things like going for overnight camping or visiting my parents.

4. Reignite Your Passions

When I had the free time I always wanted, I had to find out what I really loved and wanted to spend most of my time doing. I completely got rid of the things that were holding me back from doing what I loved. After decades of being super busy with school, work, social life, and family, I didn't know what my true passions were. It was not until I had the free time to try new things that I discovered this (I got into painting, started a blog, and started reading more again) soon I found out what I truly loved. I am into art. I love to read and write. Now that I have decluttered my schedule, I can easily do these things, whenever I want to.

5. Look for Something Deeper

The thought of traveling the world was very exciting to me in the beginning. When I actually started doing it, I felt like it was much more rewarding when I could actually share my experiences. I started writing about what I had learned on my blog, and how minimalism changed my life and led me to follow my goals that I'd pushed so far away for a long time. Today, I'm living my life happy and satisfied, knowing that I always do something that will not only enhance my life as well as the others.

6. Learn How to Say NO

It seems like 24 hours a day is not enough to do what we want and need to do. We have to acknowledge that even though there are a lot of things we can do, we don't have to do them all at the same time. Saying no to the things that are not a priority can be hard at first, but it's possible and also fulfilling. Eventually, I made a massive goal of going on a big travel trip with my family, which made my priorities much clearer and made it much easier to say no to happy hour or social events that did not help me acquire to this goal.

Saying "Yes" is Not Always Saying Yes

Saying "yes" to all things actually means that you have time for nothing. You cannot possibly say yes to everything, or else there wouldn't be enough time for you to do all the things that are important. I mean, how could you possibly get all your work don, meet everyone you have to meet up with all at the same time? Your days will be so hectic, you would not be able to rest, and more so, you would not be able to do the things that are more important.

Saying yes doesn't necessarily mean you're saying yes – it just means you can't manage your time and set your priorities right and make some serious commitments.

Take this approach: if you find it hard to say "YES!!!" in an enthusiastic way, then, it probably means no. BUT other people don't know that! So, you must learn how to be straightforward.

Say no to more, and make your life simpler.

Ask questions before filling up your calendar

Every time you look at your calendar, don't look for tasks you can remove in place of another. Instead, choose what things are important enough to stay. Ask yourself these important questions:

- ❖ Is this thing important for me enough to improve my life?
- ❖ Is this the most important thing I should do at this specific moment?
- ❖ Does this get me closer to my priorities/goals?
- ❖ Is there something more productive that I need to be doing?

Decline requests for your time

Separate your decision from your relationship. Just because you say no to something doesn't mean the person who asks you the question isn't important to you.

Have present boundaries. This may just mean that Saturdays are meant to be spent with family or using your Friday night to finish some of your assignments. Be firm with your boundaries. Yes, it might not be easy, but in the end, it'll do you a lot better and also teach you how to value people's time.

Keep in mind that when you are focused, you will be able to accomplish more things. There are times when we are asked to get involved in something, we say yes even though we are busy because we think that we can still "squeeze" it in. But remember you want to try and declutter your schedule, not fill it up. It's important to limit what you allow on your calendar, and only put in things that really matter.

How to say "no" so that you won't offend people?

"I appreciate it for asking me, but unfortunately, I won't be able to go."

"I'm sorry, but I'm occupied during that time. I'll be free on Wednesday next week, though."

"I'm honored that you would like my help, but I'm not in a situation to give it the time it deserves."

"I'm sorry, but I'm busy doing something else at that time and it's very important."

"Thank you for inviting me! However, I already have plans with my family, so I will have to pass on that one, sorry."

You can always say "no" in a nice way without offending the other person.

People can easily understand "yes" and "no", but saying "maybe", that's something you should avoid!

Saying maybe can lead to a big disappointment on their side. A vague question is no better than ditching them after saying yes. If you are not sure, ask them for more time to think about it. Tell them you will get back to them after a day or two to see whether you can make it or not.

If you are aware that you have previous engagements and you just can't make it, just let them know right away. It isn't fair to the person who is waiting for you to say yes who will only be disappointed when you don't answer.

Chapter 7

A LIFE OF ABUNDANCE

Last year, I went on a trip with my wife to Cambodia. As you know, this country is a developing nation. But you know what amazed me about this country? Their people! You see, most locals I met during my stay sit on the poverty line, and even though they have few possessions, they were the most joyful people I've ever met.

The little kids I had met were the happiest and most appreciative children I have ever encountered. And for many of them, instead of playing with toys, they were forced to work at an early age in order to survive. This is something you will hardly see in western culture.

Seeing the joy in their eyes despite the fact that they had almost nothing, made me realize how I give too much importance to material things while there are more things in the world that can bring me so much joy. This is how I learned the concept of living abundantly.

For many, living abundantly usually means living with everything taken care of for you, by your physical attachments. You have a huge closet full of clothes you never wear, gadgets you barely use, and other material things you never really use at all.

According to the dictionary, abundance means overflowing or fullness. Our lives are usually overflowing with different things, and while most of us already have all our basic needs and a little bit more we still don't seem to stop accumulating more and more things. We never become content with what we already have and what's worse, we still complain.

On the other hand, a minimalism lifestyle gives the phrase "abundant life" a positive meaning.

We can live abundantly by aiming for and enjoying things that are not physical. This could mean living a life that is full of love, adventures, peace, purpose, challenge wisdom, comfort, or anything that money couldn't easily buy.

One of the most common clichés we always hear is "*live your life*". The phrase can mean two different things. First one is to live your life to the fullest, and second, is to do whatever you want without fear. When we're *living our lives*, we usually experience joy or experience the feeling of harmony or freedom.

But the truth is that whenever we choose to 'live our life to the fullest doing anything we want without fear', we as humans will fill our lives with, material things, things that we think bring us joy, a figment of freedom. This is not how to live abundantly in minimalist perspective; this is living life with anything to make it feel abundant.

I'd say that it's the most difficult part – we are being molded by society to believe that we're living the abundant life with things. And by things, I don't mean only the material things. These things could also be pride, success, or a relationship. This makes you see material things and happiness synonymous – this makes you think that you cannot have life without stuff, just like how you can't have stuff without life.

At first glance, the idea of minimalism may seem contradictory to the word abundance. However, by looking deeper into it, you will realize how abundance and minimalism are actually closely connected – they even go hand-in-hand – in the starting a truly meaningful life.

As minimalists, we're opposed to superfluous excess… Abundance, however, is a totally different thing. The idea behind excess and abundance are the same, certainly, but abundance comes with a deeper definition: "overflowing fullness." I never liked overflowing stuff, but overflowing fullness can possibly be attained by getting rid of some of your stuff. And it's absolutely wonderful.

Starting a habit of getting rid of material things which never served us a purpose can make space for true abundance. We are making an opportunity for overflowing fullness to come into our lives.

In this next part of the book we are going to take a look into three types of abundance that we enjoy by means of embracing minimalism.

Spiritual Abundance

Our journey to living a simpler life and embracing the minimalism lifestyle was actually an answered prayer. It started 7 years ago when I lost my job and my wife was about to give birth to our first boy. Desperate, me and my wife and I decided to sell everything we knew we could live without to settle our expenses until I got a job again – after all, all we wanted is to have a good happy life. And when my first child was born, I came to a realization that I am willing to lose everything else in my life, just to make my wife and our child happy. Stuff, and old expectations I had for having "the good life" started flying out the door, and as my physical comforts decreased, my genuine happiness increased.

The following couple of years have been madly stretched and abundant in a spiritual sense. As we have relied less on material things for comfort and depended less on social norm (the idea that a bigger house, more money, the latest devices are important) our contentment has thrived. My wife and I discovered spiritual heights that were buried under all the unnecessary things we thought we had to keep.

Relational Abundance

We downsized so that we can pay bills and afford the baby's needs. The driving force behind us to choose to live simpler is so that we can live an abundant life together, as a family. Every single day, I manage to have time to build loving relationships with my wife and my kids. I get to support my wife with her passions, and we're deliberate about making enough time to build on our marriage as well as friendship. Even beyond that, my social circle is richer as I have had the flexibility to meet with my friends and relatives. Deciding to live a simpler life has provided a resilient platform for all these relationships to thrive as it allows me to spend less time and energy on worrying on complete appliances or our smartphones not being the latest model.

Creative Abundance

How we see creativity is usually limited to the fine arts: painting, music, sculpture, poetry, song, dance. For me, on the other hand, words are my expression of choice. But even though I've been running my blog for years and I wrote several books as a ghostwriter, I still experience writer's block as finding inspiration can still be a struggle. I set aside some time to have moments of white space each day to allow my soul to breathe, but a lot of times, the creativity that bubbles up out of that beautiful emptiness finds an expression I did not expect. I sing while doing a chore. I doodle on my notebook while on the train. I encourage my kids to try new things that will highlight their creativity. All of these small expressions of creativity carry a delightful joy to my day.

The purpose of minimalism is to release unnecessary things so that truly essential and beautiful things in life can shine through. When you have a lot of things to deal with, managing them all can steal your time, peace of mind, relationship, and creativity. That's something you shouldn't let happen.

Chapter 8

MINIMALISM MAINTENANCE

Organization and minimalism go hand in hand. Having a well-organized space is in flow with getting rid of the excess, which is an important step to minimalism. However, maintaining it is another thing and something that many people who are trying to live a minimalism lifestyle struggle with.

One of the most common phrases I hear from people who have started to declutter is, "I successfully declutter my space, but after a week or so, my place turned back to how it was." Same things go with the people who tried to change their habits – after a while, they find themselves doing the same things they are trying to get rid of.

Some habits are very difficult to get rid of. They may work for a while, but there is a great chance you go back to the same things you were doing.

Take dieting for example. We always hear from dieticians and nutritionists that a *"crash diet doesn't work."* This is because this particular way of dieting encourages you to eat less – or skip particular meals – for only a certain period of time until you get rid of the excess weight you want to shed. And while this diet can really be effective in helping you lose weight, there's a big chance that you will regain your weight back, if not, more.

Why does it happen?

This is because the diet encourages you to have a short-term goal, a short-cut to the goal you want to achieve. Okay, say you lose weight for doing the crash diet – you finally reach the weight you wanted, what now? You are likely to celebrate by eating a lot. Eating the food you missed during your diet. Without knowing it, you're slowly getting back to your old habits of eating unhealthy food.

So, how do you actually lose weight?

One of the most effective ways of losing weight and becoming healthy is changing your lifestyle completely. There are types of diet that will allow you to still eat the food you enjoy while making you lose weight and maintain it. Most dieticians suggest a diet that you can stay consistent with for a longer period of time, or even for good – something that will not deprive you from your natural desires and from what your body needs.

The same thing applies when maintaining minimalism. Minimalism is not meant to deprive you of your comfort, but instead, to help you see how living less can also give you comfort in a more meaningful way.

Just like crash dieting, decluttering or minimalism lifestyle, in general, doesn't stop with you, cleaning your place and getting rid of the old stuff you no longer use. It's a lifelong commitment for minimalist, which means, a change of your lifestyle, on the whole, is necessary.

8.1 Ways to Maintain Your Minimalist Lifestyle Permanently

- ✓ **Be picky about the things you allow in your house**

When you are picky when it comes to what you let inside your house, you're going to facilitate your intentional life. What are the things that are important in your life? What are the things that can really help you improve your life?

Example: If you're running a craft business and it's something you really love to do, it's natural that you'll be needing supplies. Bringing in new supplies for your craft that you need to use is part of your intentional living.

Now, if you're not a crafter and you're considering bringing crafts into your house, then you must reconsider as they are just likely to be clutter to your home.

✓ Be tough when it comes to keeping the clutter out

There's no room for laziness and procrastination when it comes to minimalism. You can save more time and energy by getting rid of all that clutter as soon as you can. Make it a routine to keeping clutter out.

Example: Whenever you finish eating, wash the dishes right away! Don't wait for later or end of the day to come before you deal with them!

✓ Be kind and polite when you refuse something

The world is full of kind and generous people, that I often find myself getting help from even when I don't really need what they're offering.

This is not an excuse to be rude to someone: you can always say no or refuse to accept something without being offensive. Or you can just simply explain to them your lifestyle and recommend giving the help to someone else who may need it more instead.

Example: Your aunt heard that you are planning to move to a new house and so she wants you to get the old sofa they no longer use. You must explain to her that you already have every piece of furniture you need, but that you know of a charity that will gladly accept it.

✓ Be confident in the lifestyle you have chosen

Let's face it…the minimalism lifestyle is not normal.

Although it's gaining popularity today due to its media exposure, it is still not widely followed. I think many people don't realize that they would actually really like minimalism if they gave it a chance. But in today's competitive society it makes it difficult for people not to desire to have better material things to show off, especially where likes and comments on social media become a measuring tool on how we are approved and perceived by others – for some, it's truly addicting.

So, because minimalism would require you to go against the norm of today's society, it's important to stand strong in this lifestyle. You can be kind and understanding to those who don't agree, but you are in no place to change them.

You can be confident that minimalism is a lifestyle that works for you!

Example: Your friend tells you you're weird for being a minimalist. You can just tell him or her that it's the lifestyle that works for you.

Most of the time, there's no point to argue and defend your lifestyle to somebody who's just trying to be rude. Some people just don't understand and it's okay. After all, you're living this lifestyle for you and not for anyone else.

Minimalism lifestyle isn't just a mindless craze. How can it be when it encourages you to make some sort of sacrifice? Generally, those who take steps to simplify and reduce their life, do it because they start to think differently about how they live their lives. Or, they see the wicked and negative nature of inconsiderate consumerism and make a mindful effort to escape this demon within themselves.

Important questions to ask yourself before you bring something new into your house:

Do you really need it?

Is it going to add value to your life?

Will it help you live the life you want?

Do you already have something that does the same purpose?

These questions will keep you from acquiring more things. These are great questions to ask yourself if you are an impulsive shopper and they worked for me 100% of the time.

8.2 Common Items to Never Buy If You Want to Have a Clutter-Free Home

On top of answering the questions mentioned above, knowing exactly the items you must avoid would be one of the best ways to have a clutter-free home – because you know they say… prevention is better than cure. Here are the items you don't want to spend your money on.

Novelty Items and Seasonal Decorations

Today, it's very easy to buy everything you think of… from a serving tray to a wind chime that has seasonal designs. But do you really need them? Getting the novelty versions of daily essentials such as soap dispensers, shower curtains, pillows, bed sheet, and cutlery, restricts their ability to be used all year round. This means they take up storage space the rest of the year when you are not planning to use them. While it might be fun to spend money on a new seasonal item, what's not fun is putting them down to store for the rest of the year. All those festive decoration items become dust-collectors. Before pulling out your wallet, ask yourself, "Is it really worth it to get these decorations for a one-day celebration?"

Trendy Clothes

Stop searching for the must-have fashion style of the season. Only because everyone else has a crop top or off-shoulder dresses, doesn't mean you must also have them in your closet. As soon as the fashion trend fades, you will just be left with even more clothes closet to declutter. Rather than following every current trend, choose the clothes you think are flattering for you and something you are comfortable wearing

Kitchen Gadgets

All the must-have, single-use, kitchen tools may seem helpful and can make your life easier until you no longer have to use them or they have stopped functioning properly. That is when they're exiled to the brimming gadget drawer that you need to declutter. A smart decluttering tip is to get multi-purpose products. So, avoid getting these kitchen gadgets that aren't worth the money and valuable space.

Organizing Solutions

Not many people realize this, but it doesn't mean that because you're buying an organizing solution, you are helping yourself to be organized. In fact, these items may just end up being new clutter. You have to be smart when buying baskets, bins, and boxes as they take up much-needed storage space in your house. Stop storing drawer organizers, containers, label makers, and other solutions. Instead, you may want to focus on trimming down the clutter so there is less stuff you need to store. This way, you won't find the need to get storage solutions.

Trendy Cookware

It seems like everyone is starting to own an air fryer. And yes, we still have that popcorn maker we hardly used because cooking popcorn in a pot is also possible. One of the best things you can do is to resist bringing home the current must-have cookware in the first place. You think you will need them, but chances are, you already have something you in your kitchen you can use as an alternative.

Craft Supplies

Bringing home crafting supplies for future crafting projects makes clutter because there's a big chance you'll never follow through on doing the project. Purchasing products to use later, even though you used a discount code or it was in a sale, is just a waste of money. You may just end up forgetting you ever bought it or deciding that you are no longer interested in doing the project. Here is a decluttering tip, whenever you feel crafty, look through your current collection of crafts and get inspiration from there.

"As Seen on TV" Items

These appealing impulse purchases get to your door in about a couple of weeks, long after the excitement to use them has passed. This just means that they may end up as clutters shoved in your drawer or sitting in the garage. Because it's too expensive to spend money on the return shipping they become one of the harder items to declutter as you paid a lot of money for them and feel guilty just throwing them out. A smart tip to remember is: just don't get them in the first place.

Freebies

And lastly, one of the known culprits for being an instant clutter is the hand-me-downs from well-meant relative, friends, and neighbors. Who doesn't like freebies, though, right? But accepting these will just give you problems later on. Are you really willing to give up storage space for all those things you didn't personally buy?

8.3 Fighting the desire

Without nurturing the minimalist mindset, minimalism can be a constant battle. You must try to resist temptations around you and reduce both of your physical and mental clutter; you try to look for natural solutions as inner urges build. Just like a crash diet, minimalism without putting your mind to it is likely to end with a big relapse. Pushing against your own desires is a losing battle.

So, if fighting against your own desires isn't what minimalism is all about, then what is it about? I'm in no place to tell you to give up all the things you have for a simpler life. I want to be as realistic as possible and to make your life a little easier. Again, remember that minimalism is about wanting less. You don't have to battle your desires. By knowing these facts, it will be easier for you to maintain this lifestyle.

Conclusion

Hopefully, this book has been helpful to you in understanding what minimalism is. Minimalist lifestyle has a different meaning for different people. But if there's one thing everyone can agree on, it is the fact that minimalism begins in the mind; it is about accepting that we don't need too much. However, it goes past more than just physical items. It goes beyond mindset, health, and even relationships.

Above all else, the best thing about minimalism is the way it benefits a person's emotional state. Rather than feeling tied down and stressed, surrounded by a home that is overflowing with unorganized things, you can embrace minimalism and reorganize your possessions in order or your home to be a place that you truly enjoy spending time in.

The benefits of minimalism can spread into all areas of your life, from decluttering your closet and feeling more organized to letting go of toxic relationships that no longer make you happy.

In many instances, minimalism also brings out the best and worst in humankind. Just look at Black Friday videos that show how modern consumerist standards are just plain wrong. Who cares about your 45-inch flat screen? Is it really worth competing getting yourself in a chaotic situation that can potentially hurt you? Remember that humans were not born to consume and become stuck in a cycle of purchasing stuff in the hopes of raising their social status or filling an emotional void.

At the end of the day, you cannot take material things to your grave — well, technically, you can, but they would not benefit your rotting corpse. So, spend your time on things that are really important in your life.

Similarly, minimalism doesn't need to be followed to the extreme. Minimalism doesn't require you to live in a little white room without belongings and sleep on the floor. More importantly, it is not a competition. For a lot of people, minimalism is the process of striving toward a simpler, more thoughtful lifestyle. Strict devotion to one set of rules, or total self-discipline, isn't required. There are no hard and fast rules.

THE MINIMALIST BUDGET MADE EASY

BY

SIMON DAVIES

Introduction

While it may come with different definitions, minimalism, for many, is a lifestyle that focuses on getting rid of the clutter in your life – both physically and mentally. Those who follow this lifestyle find that getting rid of the distractions in their lives gives them more opportunities to enjoy different aspects of life. And while minimalist lifestyle comes with many benefits, what many people enjoy the most about it is how it helps them manage their finances better.

Embracing minimalism doesn't mean that you're going to have to stop using money completely; it just means that you have to only spend money on things that can improve your life.

If you win the lottery, what would you do with the money? For most people, the first things they might think about are material things. It could be a new iPhone, a luxury car, or just anything that would make them look rich – probably to impress people who they don't even like. This wouldn't be the case for a minimalist. If a minimalist wins the lottery, he would think twice or maybe more than twice before spending his money on material things.

In this book, you will learn what a minimalist would probably buy if he wins a lottery, and even when he doesn't. You will learn where it is worth spending your money, from the perspective of a minimalist – i.e., from my perspective.

But my perception wasn't always like this.

Like many people, I used to think that money should be my number one priority as an adult. As a result, I sacrificed a lot and spent most of my life making money. I spent many hours risking my health, neglecting the people that I care about, and abandoning the things that made me genuinely happy. The more I forgot these things, the more important the money became. But even though people saw me happy and contented, I felt a lot of things were missing.

I made a good amount of money during my days in the corporate world, but ironically, that lifestyle made me spend a lot of money. And I believe that it was one of the main sources of my dissatisfaction, one that haunted me during my twenties.

When I was twenty, I worked 6 or 7 days a week, and I earned a little over $50,000 a year, which was a lot of money, considering I didn't have a degree. And again, the problem was that when I was earning 50 grand, I was spending 60 grand; the more I earned, the more I spent. Later on, I had worked my way up to a higher position, leading me to work literally 362 days a year, and I was earning in six figures. While it sounds great, I was still spending more money than I was bringing home.

So, instead of bringing home an impressive salary, I just was able to bring home anxiety, debt, and devastating amount of unhappiness. My love and hate relationship with money was, actually, my biggest root of unhappiness.

I know I deserve to be labeled as stupid. But it's not because I was wasting my hard-earned income, but because I valued it more than I should. You could say that I worshipped it.

Thanks to minimalism, however, my perspective on money has truly changed. Minimalism has helped me get rid of the excess in order for me to focus on things that are truly important. And now, at 32, I make less money than I did when I was younger. But at least I can afford everything I need, I'm not in debt, I'm don't get anxiety, and most importantly, I feel contented.

Now, when spending money on anything, I ask myself one question: *Is this worth my hard work?*

Is this shirt worth $50 of my time?

Is this meal worth $15 of my time?

Is this smartphone worth $1000 of my time?

By doing this, I can make sure that every cent I spend adds huge value to my life. I have a roof over my head, food in my stomach, clothes to keep me warm, and little things that make my life more comfortable.

Chapter 1

WHAT IS A MINIMALIST?

Before we talk about minimalist budgeting, let's talk about minimalism. Then we will discuss how it is different from the form of budgeting you're probably used to.

Again, the definition of minimalism may vary from person to person. Some people relate it to music and art, while others relate this word to architectures and interior design. I can't even find a dictionary that relates it to a lifestyle choice, so, let me define this word how I see it, as someone who is a self-proclaimed minimalist.

Minimalism is a lifestyle which involves living with only things and thoughts that are necessary for bringing happiness, health, and general well-being.

I choose to take a softer approach to a minimalist lifestyle. For me, it's more of a journey than a destination. For some, it is about living with 5 pieces of clothes or living with a minimal amount of clutter in their house.

But don't worry; minimalism is not about doing it hardcore – you don't have to reduce your possessions below a certain amount. Owning less than 50 items in your household shouldn't be your goal. Your goal is to reach the level where you are comfortable – if you want to reduce the number of your possessions, make sure that it's going to benefit you rather than make your life inconvenient.

In today's society where it's all about buying the latest fancy things, it can be a real challenge to imagine that having less stuff could be more beneficial to us. I mean, do you know anyone who would say no to a nice, big house or the latest gadgets? While there might be nothing wrong with it for some people, the fact that you're reading this might possibly mean that you've noticed how your material possessions are no longer bringing you happiness. If this is the case, then you might be ready to get more from less.

1.1 Why Less Is More

There's no denying that most of us own a great amount of excess in our lives –too much stuff, too many expenses, too many responsibilities, and too many commitments. Can you really still enjoy life despite this chaos? Do you sometimes wish you could simply push a button and turn your life around and make it more fun and relaxing? You are able to make a haven of peace not only for yourself, but you can also turn your expectations into reality. Let's bust one of the myths about minimalism – *Minimalism is all about having less stuff.*

This is the most common misconception about minimalism! Yes, for most, minimalism is about getting rid of the material things that no longer bring joy into your life, which can also deter you from moving forward.

However, minimalism is not only about material things; it could also be about having less responsibilities and fewer things to worry about. And in this subchapter, let's talk about how your schedule and responsibilities can be minimized as well.

If you do or have many things that no longer benefit or support you on a long-term basis, then getting rid of them would be a better and more beneficial choice than keeping them. But of course, it's impossible to get rid of everything – if you throw away, lessen, reduce, and remove as much as you can, you're forming a void in your life. The goal of minimalism is just to show you the truly important things in the world.

In order to understand what has to be removed and what has to be added, you can look at your activities and material things as either assets or liabilities.

Assets

An asset is something that's worth some value. If you are familiar with terms used in finance, then you know examples of assets include stocks, buildings, bonds, gold, land, etc., but we can look at assets a bit more broadly. An asset could be anything that:

- ❖ Upturns in value
- ❖ Offers something valuable like money and happiness
- ❖ Toughens and empowers you
- ❖ Takes you closer to your goals
- ❖ Offers positivity and excitement
- ❖ Calms and relaxes you
- ❖ Improves health and energy

Liabilities

Liabilities, on the other hands, are debts, obligations, and things that are worth more money than they yield. But again, let's look at it more broadly. Liability can be anything that:

- ❖ Takes from you
- ❖ Lowers in value
- ❖ Removes or lessens something valuable like money, security, joy, happiness, etc.
- ❖ Makes you weak
- ❖ Keeps you from attaining your goals
- ❖ Offers undesirable stress
- ❖ Produces anxiety or agitates
- ❖ Declines health and energy

So, in short, assets give, while liabilities take.

Now, how is this relevant to minimalism? To show you its relevance clearly, let's do a little exercise.

Make a list of all things in your life – from people that are close to you, projects you are planning to make, and all the commitments you have in your life, including expenses, goals, and belongings. Because this can be a handful task, you can make it simpler by focusing on one area first – one at a time List each of your responsibilities, commitments, obligations, or whatever you want to call them. If you are having a tough time remembering, you can take out a calendar and look back a few months and then carefully forward a few months to help refresh your memory. Make your list as big as you can. Your list may include random responsibilities like mowing the lawn, homeowner's association meeting, paying bills, taking dogs to the vet, volunteering, shopping for groceries, driving the kids to school, meeting your friends on weekends, etc.

Once you're done with your list, you can then categorize each of these commitments as either a LIABILITY or an ASSET. Does the responsibility or activity listed give or take? Does it help you attain the goals and dreams you have? Does it bring you joy or just stresses you out?

Now that you're done sorting them out, what you have to do next is to see if you can eliminate any of the ones listed as LIABILITY. It's impossible to get rid of all the items listed as a liability. However, still, try to get rid of as many as you can. The goal of this exercise is to make you conscious of what gives and takes, which in turn can help you make decisions about what responsibilities you can add to assets and what responsibilities you can get rid of completely.

Doing more might generate more money in your life, but ask yourself… are you really happy? Is money really more important than your happiness, health, and overall well-being? Doing less is likely to give you more: more time, more opportunities to enjoy life, and more joy.

Less Is More as Your Mantra

Integrating minimalism in every aspect of your life can bring in serenity and tranquillity. Making a space that is going to motivate you to relax and making your home a sanctuary will guarantee that will help you prioritize your needs. Similarly, focusing on activities that feed your soul and bring contentment into your life is a form of minimalism that could benefit each one of us.

Following the idea behind *'less is more'* can create a haven for your home, where you are able to recharge your batteries and get yourself ready for the next day's activities while enjoying time with things you like and people you love.

1.2 Signs You Be A Minimalist In The Making

If you have been minimalizing your life or considering starting to live your life as a minimalist, then congratulations. My actions screamed minimalism long before my brain registered that I am actually trying to live as a minimalist. Read on for some tell-tale signs that you probably have the heart of a minimalist.

1. You organize all aspects of your life, and it's so therapeutic for you. You either live a laboriously tidy life or at least want to. Making lists has become a habit for you: shopping lists, to-do lists, guest lists, etc. Whenever you can see ideas and plans visibly in front of you, you feel in control, and even the hardest tasks are achievable. Presented with mess and disorder, you become disheartened.

2. You want to look presentable all the time, but you don't fuss too much over how you look. Unless it is your wedding day, you would hardly be all dressed up. No matter what the occasion is, you'd rather wear shoes that make you feel comfortable and look natural with just enough makeup to make you feel confident.

3. In terms of clothing, you're into signature pieces that embody your personality and are made of high-quality materials – the flawlessly fitting jeans, a gorgeous couturier blazer, the classic bag. You may yield to the brief temptation of fun current trends. However, you may look at them as cheap thrills instead of investments.

4. You appreciate quality and the sophisticated things and get little to no satisfaction from lower-quality alternatives. You'd rather save up and spend $80 buying a good quality jacket, instead of buying a $30 one that is made to look exactly the same. You are attracted to fine craftsmanship and quality.

5. Wastes disgust you. Most of your makeup can last you for years, you reluctantly use up that final centimetre of pencil, and you stubbornly excerpt 'cost for wear-out of all the pieces of clothing – which usually means getting creative with upcycling or repurposing the pieces that are no longer in style.

6. Cleanliness and functionality attract you more than the overly ornamental. So, of course, you attracted towards cleanliness, simple textures, and neutral colours.

7. You value space extremely. You'd rather have a house that has no furniture and sit on the floor like Japanese do, instead of filling all parts of your house. This doesn't mean that your home is bland or doesn't have any personality. It's actually quite far from it – since you choose all your stuff carefully, your home is a unique extension of what kind of person you are or what qualities you carry.

8. In terms of money, you're not tight with money, but at the same time, you don't spend too much money. You would not feel hesitant to spend four digits on something you really like, but of course, you'll make sure you are getting the best quality your money can get. You love a bargain, and the % sign makes you excited.

9. Clutter is one of the things that grind your gear, so routine cleaning is something you treat as a hobby instead of a chore. Getting rid of the superfluous gives you satisfaction, as well as simplifies your life and helps you reconsider your priorities.

10. Your hatred towards clutter extends to people around you. You choose to surround yourself with those who matter most to you or those who benefit your life. So, deleting friends on Facebook who you don't connect with has become a habit for you.

Chapter 2

A Minimalist's Approach to Money

What Is Minimalist Budgeting?

Now that you probably have a better understanding as to what a minimalist is, let's now talk about what it has to do with money.

Generally, minimalism means giving value to things that are essential, while purposely getting rid of the clutter in your life. While the first thing that comes to one's mind when decluttering are material things like clothes, furniture, and other house clutter, minimalism can also be applied to your financial life.

A minimalist budget will provide you clarity on how to manage your money by decluttering your finances and putting your financial goals as your priority.

One warning that is worth mentioning, however, is that a minimalist budget does not necessarily mean you will have to spend less money. You are able to just simplify your finances while still spending a great amount of money on something that is important.

Frugality is not the same as minimalist budgeting. These two concepts are significantly different – I'll explain further in the following chapter in order for you to see what I am talking about.

However, by reducing the clutter and confusion in your financial life, you will become very aware of how you are treating your finances. By doing this, you're increasing your awareness of excessive spending. And having that awareness is the first step to changing your financial lifestyle.

2.1 What the Minimalist Budget Is Not

The minimalist budgeting will keep you from maximizing your credit card for rewards, deals, coupons, or other consumer freebies that involve subscribing to multiple accounts, which will cost you more money in the long run.

The minimalist budgeting would not save you the most dollars or turn you into the most frugal person.

Instead, the minimalist budgeting is going to help you make your finances simpler in order for you to have an easier system that helps you attain your financial objectives and in turn, makes your life easier.

I see how it made a huge difference in my life. I stopped using a credit card, which makes my life easier and more worry-free. I no longer spend money more than I have to. I have my debit card, which I use for most purchases I make. This means that I no longer benefit from the perks, bonuses, and discounts I get from using a credit card, but I don't think they are worth it, anyway. I do this for the sake of getting rid of clutter and temptation. It works for me perfectly.

Minimalist budgeting taught me the importance of sticking to what's essential in life.

It helped me and still helping me live my life in a simpler manner while still having enough money to live a comfortable life but cutting down financial responsibilities. Minimalism has made the quality of my life better not only financially but also mentally.

2.2 Minimalist Living vs. Frugal Living

Again, it's important to understand that minimalist living and frugal living are two different things.

Minimalist living is about choosing to own less stuff, while the frugal living is about spending less money on buying stuff.

By knowing the difference between the two, you will have clarity and focus on what matters the most to you, which in turn, helps you make better decisions when it comes to money.

But let's get deeper and talk about this topic further to make sure that you understand the concept behind these two things.

What is Frugal Living?

Frugal living is a lifestyle that centers on making the most of every cent you spend. It is about being thrifty with the money, like searching for the best deals and promos and using coupons or voucher codes. People who are frugal aim to spend as less money as possible.

Another quality that a frugal person usually has, unlike a minimalist, is having a lot of stuff. Most frugal individuals own a lot of stuff that they were able to acquire at a good price.

A frugal shopper: "I bought these towels at the mall today. They are of average quality, but they were on sale. Now, I have a lot more in my storage in case I'll need them later."

For many people who follow the frugal living, their argument focuses only on getting the best deal their money can get. Frugal living can bring about a lot of clutter and stuff that are not necessary for your life that you can find yourself attached to.

Now, What Is Minimalist Living?

Minimalist living, on the other hand, is a lifestyle that focuses on acquiring fewer things. People who are minimalists want to own a few but excellent-quality items that make their life better – and they don't care if they have to spend more money on them.

The goal of minimalism is how we can improve the quality of life by not owning a lot of belongings. It is about getting rid of excess and clutter and giving focus on things that don't matter.

A minimalist shopper: "I just got a new pair of gym shoes that make my training more comfortable and improve my overall performance. They're pretty expensive, but they are the only pair of gym shoes I have, so it's worth it."

I'm a minimalist at heart. I always find myself eliminating a lot of stuff I no longer need. I don't get too attached to my things anymore. The thought of having more stuff gives me anxiety. I'd rather spend more money on something that is more high-quality.

But is it possible to be both?

While there are a lot of differences between minimalism and frugality, please note that they are NOT exclusive. This means that you can be both at the same time.

The frugal-minimalist, as I call it, is the ultimate powerhouse. This person would rather spend less money when he purchases something, and at the same time, would look for the best quality his money can buy, and he also doesn't want to buy a lot. He minds the quality but would think twice before buying anything. He gives importance to his money; overspending is the last thing he would do. He also doesn't want for his house to be filled with too many things.

The frugal-minimalist is almost perfect when it comes to his spending, saving, and owning. It may be impossible to be this perfect, but we can try and fight against our natural urges, whether to spend more or own more!

2.3 How to Be More Frugal and More of A Minimalist

The lifestyle one follows vary from person to person. Now, let me share with you how I try to live as a frugal-minimalist.

To live frugally,

- ❖ Avoid buying at full price
- ❖ Buy at discount and thrift stores
- ❖ Subscribe to deal sites
- ❖ Use vouchers or coupons
- ❖ Buy second-hand

- Live below your means
- Buy in bulk
- Choose to stay at home on weekends

To live as a minimalist,

- Only buy something when you know you really need it
- Don't buy something just because it is cheap
- Always give importance to quality rather than quantity
- Learn how to let go of things when they are no longer in use
- Remove emotional attachments to material things
- Know what brings real happiness to your life

Now, you know that minimalist living and frugal living are two different mindsets. Again, the former focuses on spending less and getting the best deal but doesn't pay much attention to quality or quantity. The latter focuses on owning fewer things and living simply, with a focus on quality and not much focus on price.

You can be both minimalist and frugal. However, you may find one comes more naturally to you. Either way, both these lifestyles can help you live more intentionally and become more satisfied and happy in the long run.

2.4 Guide to Spending Money as a Minimalist

Because the idea of minimalism is living life with less in order to simplify your life, it comes with the idea of being intentional about purchasing less stuff and bringing less stuff into your home. And don't get me wrong, of course, minimalists still need to go shopping and purchase things. The idea behind learning how to shop like a minimalist is to be intentional about what you spend your money on. Being intentional with your shopping decisions lets you avoid a clutter-filled home. So, now, let me give you some strategies that will help you shop like a minimalist and encourage you to make intentional purchases.

Moderate Minimalist

If there are levels of minimalism, this is the category I fall into. But what do I mean when I say Moderate Minimalist? This is someone working hard to decrease and get rid of anything he doesn't need or love in his home. But at the same time, he's someone who is not willing to live with so little that he foregoes things that give him a convenient and comfortable life that makes him happy.

As I've said before, minimalism looks different for each of us. It is about finding a balance between too much and too little. That point of balance is anywhere that is "enough" for you. It's a place where your life is minimized and simplified to the point where you just keep the things in your home you use on a regular basis and those things make you truly happy.

Figuring out what adds Value to Your Life

For me, personally, I don't believe that to live a successfully minimalist life, you have to be restrictive on what you let yourself buy. Instead, having a minimalist mind-set and knowing how to shop like a minimalist is about being intentional with what you buy and what you bring into your home. When you find yourself at a store and see something that captures your attention, for example, a nice pair of shoes, ask yourself, do you really need it, or you're just considering buying it because you think it would look good on you? If the reason is the latter, then walk away. Shopping intentionally means prioritizing purpose over aesthetics.

We usually carefully think through our bigger purchases before making them. But it's usually the small things we buy here and there, that do not seem like a lot or don't seem like a big deal, or something that could clutter up our home. By teaching ourselves to shop like a minimalist, we can successfully live a more comfortable life and at the same time, use our money wisely.

To effectively spend money as a minimalist, I've put up a 2-part strategy that will guide you. The first part of these strategies focuses on ways to change your general mind-set and shopping behaviour to shop like a minimalist. It intends to help you become more intentional regarding what you purchase and what's your reason for buying it. On the other hand, the second part focuses on questions to ask yourself when you've decided to purchase something. These are strategies to check in with yourself and make sure that the purchase will really add value to your life.

Part 1: Different Ways to Shop Intentionally

These are ideas you can implement before you go shopping. They're general questions and strategies that are likely to change the way you buy things. These are meant to help you be deliberate and intentional with your purchases and start to shop in a minimalist manner.

This, in turn, will slow the inbound flow of clutter into your home, helping you make sure that everything you are buying and bringing into your home will be valuable and not just another addition to clutter.

1. Unsubscribe from store email lists

Getting rid of temptations is one of the best ways to avoid impulsive shopping. These businesses are advertisement champs, and they're good at what they do! It could be difficult to resist the temptation to buy when your inbox is filled with emails telling you about their promotions and latest products.

You are much more likely to make intentional purchases when you search for the item, instead of buying them just because they were offered to you.

2. Stop going to the malls and shopping centres

The same idea as controlling your email applies to this. If you spend too much time in malls or shopping places, the extremely effective marketing and advertising of the retailers will persuade you to check out their products and you might end up buying them.

If you try to avoid malls and shopping places, you can avoid the ever-effective marketing and pressure to make a purchase.

3. Research all the available options earlier

Before buying anything, search for possible options available online. Make sure to read feedback and reviews from people who have tried the product before. Look into the pros and cons of every item you want to buy.

There are times we all get captivated in the idea of needing to own something new. Doing research about it in advance can help you figure out if the item is actually something you need and if it's even worth your money.

4. Wait for the next day before purchasing

Many of us buy things in an impulse, which eventually leads to regret. In order to avoid this, you may want to wait at least 24 hours before deciding to buy the item. This will give you enough time to think if it's really worth it, or it's just going to end up being useless later.

5. Take it a step further and wait longer

If you want something that you know you don't really need but still want to buy it, then maybe stay a little bit patience and wait for a little longer. If there is something you want to buy, write it down and wait up to 30 days before buying it. If 30 days pass and you still want to buy it, then maybe you it's a wise decision to buy it.

6. Plan a no-spending day/week/month

Freezing your spending is a great way to shed some light on your spending and buying practices. This way, you cannot just save money, but you'll also have the chance to see how considerately or inconsiderately you make purchases.

7. Fairly evaluate your intentions in wanting to buy something new

Before making any purchase, honestly evaluate the reason for you for buying it in the first place. Is it because you know that it's going to add value into your life, or is it because you just want to get on with the trend? Do you just want to make yourself feel better buying something new? Are you just buying it because you want to impress people you don't even like?

Many times, many people buy something for the wrong reason. Start shopping like a minimalist by always being honest with yourself about what your motivation is for buying something.

8. Make a list and stick to it

After doing your research, have some time to think and ask yourself if you are buying for the right reasons. Make a list of what you need to buy and stick to it.

9. Pay with cash

This has been very effective for me, and I encourage everyone who wants to control their spending to do this. Instead of using a credit card or debit card, use cash. This is how your mind works -- when you pay in cash, you will be mindful and aware that the money in your pocket is already running out.

10. Choose experience over material things

If you were to choose between a brand new phone and a plane ticket to a place you haven't been before for the weekend, what would you choose? For some, it's so easy to choose the phone, arguing that it lasts for years while traveling to a new place will last for a few days. However, to live a minimalist life, you'd be encouraged to give more value to experience or something consumable to buy instead of a material thing that will just add clutter to your space.

Some examples of these experience and consumable gifts include, but are not limited to, concert tickets, lesson fees, museum passes, restaurant gift checks, groceries, etc. These are very thoughtful and personalized gifts, and more importantly, they wouldn't add clutter to your home.

11. Wear out or use up your things before replacing it

Before even considering buying something new, see first if the thing you currently have is already replaceable. This helps me drastically in eliminating the duplicates that bring clutter to your home.

12. Follow the one in, one out rule

If you want to keep your home free from clutter, this would be a great way to shop like a minimalist. This keeps clutter in check, so it does not build back in your home. Every time you bring something new into your home, look for something you may want to get rid of in place of it. Or better, look for two things you may want to get rid of in order to further lessen any clutter in your house.

Part 2: How to Buy with Intention

In this second part, we will talk about some of the important questions to ask yourself when you've finally decided to buy something. These strategies are going to help you to carefully and deliberately consider the purchase before making it, to make sure it is going to add value to your life.

1. Do you really need it?

Be honest with yourself about what you really need to buy. If the answer is not an absolute yes, then you may want to re-evaluate your decision.

2. Can you leave without it?

Again, be honest with yourself if you can go on with your life without the item you are considering to buy. There are times we can get very excited about the idea of owning something new. Or settle for something that's not really worth it just because we want something new. If you know you can get by without it, or it's not an inconvenience not owning it, then maybe ditch it.

3. Where are you going to put the item?

In order to avoid more clutter, one of the best solutions you will have is to find a place for them. Finding a place where things can easily be accessed is necessary to keep them from turning into clutter. If you can't think of any place to put the items after buying them, then hold off buying them until you get a place or space in your house where you can put them.

4. How often will you use them?

How essential the item is in your daily life? If you'll use it often and it is going to add value to your life while you're doing it, then it's probably worth your money. On the other hand, if it is something you're only going to use sometimes, then leave it. Not to mention, if you buy it, you will have to keep it, maintain it, and clean it, but you would not actually use it frequently.

5. Do you already have something that you can use instead?

With your creativity and wit, you might see that you already have something you could use instead of the item you want to buy.

Whether it is a piece of garment or a kitchen gadget, if you already have something similar or something that serves the same purpose you are looking for, you might not have to buy something new after all.

6. What's something you're willing to let go in replacement of something you are planning to buy?

Remember the one in, one out rule I mentioned earlier? You must choose what you are willing to get rid of for the new item you are planning to buy.

And remember to always stick to this rule. After buying, get rid of the item you are willing to let go and either throw it away, donate it, or sell it.

2.5 Intention over Restriction

I'm not saying that you cannot have any fun shopping or ever treat yourself to buy something new. It isn't about restricting yourself to the point that it makes you feel stressed out and unhappy.

Actually, it is supposed to give you the opposite effect! Again, the point of learning how to shop like a minimalist is to become more intentional with the things you buy and bring into your household, to avoid cluttering your home and space with stuff that is not adding value to your life.

The goal is to give yourself more space, time, and freedom to live life to the fullest and to enable you to live a life filled with the most important things: the people you truly care about.

I know that it might not always be "fun" to say no to buying more or getting the latest stuff. However, learning to shop like a minimalist is surely going to recompense in the long run when you realize that your home is uncluttered and very liveable. When you're not spending your free time organizing and cleaning the things you own, instead of doing something else more important, then you will get the reward for a minimalistic life.

The intentional shopping choices you make right now will let you spend your weekend afternoons doing something you enjoy and love instead of cleaning your whole house over and over again.

Again, as I said earlier, everyone, including serious minimalists, need to buy new things from time to time. Things get worn out and broken and might need a replacement. However, when you know how to shop like a minimalist and how to embrace a minimalist mind-set, you will also know the difference between buying things mindlessly and buying something that is truly worth it. And purchasing things after careful consideration and making a thoughtful decision to buy derived from the value is going add value to your life.

2.6 The 50/30/20 Rule of Budgeting

Budgeting is not only about having enough money to pay your bills and being able to pay them on time – budgeting should about determine how much you must be spending and on what. The 50/20/30 rule of budgeting is a comparative guideline that is able to help you keep your spending in alliance with your savings goals.

Adults are able to benefit significantly from following the simple ideologies set forth by this rule of budgeting. As long as you know how to attain a stable budget, you are able to take the next steps to further modify this rule around your own unique goals and expenses.

The 50/20/30 budgeting rule can particularly help young adults who are starting to deal with the tricky world of finance. By making an effort of getting into this system, budgeting, in general, would be an easy thing for you to deal with. Of course, you can always make adjustments based on your lifestyle and preferences. However, by keeping yourself close to the core idea of this budgeting system, you are guaranteed to gain financial ground, instead of losing it.

50% of Your Income – Essentials

To start following this rule, allocate no more than half of your income for the absolute necessities in your life. This might seem like a high fraction of your income, but when you consider all things that fall into this category, it starts to make a little more sense.

To make it clear, what I mean by essential expenses are those ones you'd almost definitely need to pay, no matter where you are living, where you are working, or what your goals are. Generally, these expenses are almost the same for everybody and include housing, food, transportation expenses, and of course, the utility bills. The fraction allows you to adjust, while still keeping a comprehensive, stable budget. And keep in mind that it is more about the total amount compared to individual costs. For example, some people are living in high-rent areas, yet are able to walk to work; similarly, others benefit from much lower housing expenses while dealing with more expensive transportation fee.

20% of Your Income – Savings

The following step is to bestow 20% of your take-home income toward savings. This includes debt payments, savings plans, and rainy-day funds – things you must add to, but which would not imperil your life or make you homeless if you did not. That is a bit of a generalization, but you get the idea. This class of expenses must only be paid after your essentials are already covered and before you even consider anything in the following category.

You can look at it as your "get ahead" category. Whereas 50% of your income is the goal for essentials, 20% – or more – must be your goal in terms of obligations. You will be able to pay off your debt faster and make more important steps toward a stress-free future by dedicating as much of your income as you can to this category.

The word "retirement" may not bring a sense of urgency when you are only in your early 20s. However, it surely will become more persistent in many years to come. Just remember that the advantage of starting while you are young is that you'll earn bigger interest the longer you allow the funds to grow.

30% of Your Income – Personal Expenses

Now, to the last category, and it is also the one that can truly make the most difference in your budget are the personal expenses you make. There are financial experts that consider this category totally optional. However, in today's world, a lot of these so-called luxuries have taken on more of an obligatory position. It all depends on what your goal in life is and what you are willing to sacrifice. The reason that this category takes a bigger fraction compared to the previous category is due to the reason that a lot of things falls into it.

These personal expenses include things like your mobile phone plan, internet bill, and trips. If you're travel expansively or work online, your mobile internet plan is possibly more of a necessity and not a luxury. But you need some wiggle room because you can choose which plan to pay for. Other things in this category include coffee shop visits, gym memberships, evenings with friends, and the like. You're the only one who can choose which of your expenses can be labelled as "personal," and which ones are really obligatory. The same as how no more than 50 % of your income must go toward vital expenses, 30% is the maximum amount you may spend on personal needs. The fewer expenses you have in this category, the more development you will make settling down your debt and working hard towards your goals.

Creating good habits will pay off in the long term. You're not required to have a high income to follow the creeds of the 50/20/30 budgeting rule; anybody can do it. Because this is a percentage-based system, similar amounts apply whether you are earning an entry-level salary and earning handsome amount of money, or if you have been working for years and have a lot of sources of income.

There's something you need to remember, though: You don't have to take this rule literally. While the proportions are sound, our lives vary from person to person. This plan does provide an outline for you to work within. When you review your income and spending and define what's important and what is not, only then you are able to make a budget that helps you make the most of your income. Many years from now, you are still able to fall back on the same guidelines to assist you with your budget as your life evolves.

Chapter 3

Avoiding Unnecessary Spending

3.1 The Psychology of Spending Money

The purpose and importance of money may vary from person to person. The way you look at money has a direct influence on what you currently have in your life and is going to be a determining factor of how much you'll inevitably draw to your life.

Why do people spend too much and why for many, curbing those impulses can be too difficult? Even though it looks simple from the outside, the truth is, the reasons behind people's spending can be rather complicated. A lot of research has shown that. Below I listed some of the main reasons that trigger people to spend and overspend.

Emotional triggers

It's human nature to want things; these wants include health, happiness, being loved, safety, and to get those things better than others. Many companies use advertising strategies that make people want to have better things than others. Alternatively, they trigger fear when selling products that claim to make your home more secure, make you safe from accidents, and prevent your body from changing negatively. Marketers study the lifestyles of the consumers and their world views to address specific psychological triggers. When successfully tapped, it's going to be hard to remain rational in the face of them.

People love a bargain

Seeing something at a reduced price makes people feel like they are smart consumers. However, it could counter your goal when you had not planned on making buying that anyway, had not yet budgeted for it, or had not planned on that much money on anything anyway!

Too many options

The more decisions you need to make, the less likely it is for you to fight temptation. According to multiple types of research, when the willpower of a person is run down, they tend to spend more money and buy more items than those who have not recently used their willpower.

According to the American Psychological Society, willpower can be compared to a muscle that gets tired after being used for a certain period. Those who are financially insecure and thus always facing hard financial decisions are at a greater risk of exhausting willpower. According to one study, for example, people who are not financially secure are more likely to purchase food and drink while shopping compared to people who are well off. There are also studies that have shown shoppers in malls are likely to make most of their purchases in the third hour of their time there.

In other words, when our willpower is exhausted, we're more likely to be persuaded by urges, desires, and cravings—even though we may regret those purchases later on.

Needs versus wants

The result of globalized trade is that the products that were used to be seen as luxury items – for example, electronics and toys – are now increasingly produced in bulk. This explosion of consumer goods has made products cheaper and less valuable. A profusion of affordable things isn't essentially a bad thing. However, it's important to know whether something is a need or a want.

Buying love

Special occasions like birthdays, Christmas Day, and anniversaries are traditional reasons to give gifts. Actually, spending during the winter holidays makes up 20% of total annual retail sales in America. Similarly, Mother's Day, Valentine's Day, Father's Day, Graduation Day, and the like, have presented themselves as reasons to give, and of course, spend money. If you associate your appreciation with the price of your gift, you're more likely to spend too much. In a world that is too materialistic, it's easy to forget how experiences and memories are far more valuable than material things.

Filling a void

Based on the research done by the University of Michigan's Ross School of Business in 2014, shopping helps people feel better. As people feel sad or deserted about a situation they've found themselves in, they claim, "retail therapy," may help people feel better. That's for the reason that the options involved in shopping can boost their sense of personal control. Shopping, just like drinking alcohol and overeating, can help some people manage their stress.

Quick thrills

Also known as "present bias," sellers take advantage of the fact that the charm of getting something today is stronger compared to the appeal of getting something later on. But of course, the problem is that instant gratification can get in the way of a person's long-term goals, even though the latter would give far more happiness in the long run. Furthermore, credit cards and online shopping have made instant gratification easier to gain more than ever.

Marketers are fully aware of the powers that influence the behaviour of consumers. As those forces hit your deepest emotions, including your dreams and fears, you can easily fall victim to at least a few of what's mentioned above.

But fortunately, the more you are aware of these forces and how they approach you, the easier it is going to be for you to deal with these changes.

It's important to think in abundance and accept that you already have enough for what you need. The key ingredient to changing the way you think of money from a harmful mind-set to a positive mind-set is to make yourself aware of the words you use. Never call yourself broke to describe your personal financial situation; instead, use tight budget or fixed income. The more you use different words of abundance to classify your situation, the more your subconscious will think that those words are true.

3.2 How to Differentiate Compulsive from Excessive Spending

You get your pay check, and you're very thrilled about it. You've planned on saving half of it in your bank account. But instead, you clicked on a little banner on your browser showing pictures of shoes you think would look good on you. You put them in your cart, and as you're browsing on the site, you saw a bag that is on sale. You put it in your cart as well thinking that if you buy it later, it might already be gone and by buying it now, you can save on shipping fee. Now you have a nice pair of shoes and a bag. You continue buying stuff even though you already have a lot of it and you will barely use the new ones and obviously, you're on the verge of reaching your credit card's maximum limit. A part of you is already panicking, but you still keep buying.

Well, I have news for you: you're a compulsive spender. This is a form of addiction that is more commonly observed in women than in men. Women can easily spend their whole pay check in one store.

There are several possible reasons for compulsive spending, and some of those reasons are temporary depression or loneliness. Some people think that compulsive spending can make them feel happy or contented, but this is not always the case. This is because even though compulsive spending gives brief pleasure, it could just actually makes your life worse.

After spending most, if not all, of your money, you might face an emergency, and you'll be left without financial help. To a great extent, it cannot only affect you, but also your family, your health, and even your job as you're always dealing with the pressure of how you're going to cope your expenses and pay bills and other things that involve financial settlement. You might have to take an extra job to settle the bills, which may impede your credit scores.

Yes, you might not be taking drugs or drinking a lot of alcohol – you're just shopping… too much. However, this extreme spending is considered as addiction, and you might have a compulsive spending disorder. It's a disorder that's completely destroying you much faster than you'd ever think of.

A compulsive spending disorder triggers you to spend more and more money on things – even if it's beyond your capacity or it's something you don't actually need. The compulsive spending disorder is a symptom that indicates that someone is extremely disturbed. Recognizing and acknowledging that you have a problem is the best way to overcome it. If you know that your compulsive spending is the reason for your problems, it is going to be easier for you to avoid it. You can always talk to a therapist. You are able to overcome the compulsive spending disorder because this ever-addictive behaviour can be treated. With some help, you can overcome this disorder.

3.3 Effective Ways to Overcome Overspending

You might be thinking that recognizing excessive personal spending is easy – when someone is shopping for many things without caring about the bill. This observation might be true, but is a threat of passing judgment, and maybe not having enough details about the person being seen. To identify that a person overspends, you need to see first his goal for buying too many things. Judging someone from another's person's perspective is not easy, but seeing it in yourself and identifying if you are overspending is easier. If you believe that you tend to overspend, then this is for you. Below is a basic plan that can immediately help you to regulate excessive spending.

1. Create a future reference by visualizing your anticipated position 3 to 5 years from now. It's a great idea to create a long-term position first before thinking of short-term to help you remain focused and more motivated.

2. List down your visualization with a header "Vision Statement" and add a projected emotional response as you trip towards fulfilment.

3. Write an achievement goal that's important to help you understand your vision in each of the following areas like social, educational, financial, and personal health.

4. Plan the dollar amount that is going to be necessary to achieve your goals and see your vision in 3 to 5 years.

5. Define your current spending pattern per month in order to see if you'll have the resources or if you'll need to make changes in order to see your vision in the following years.

This step by step method will help you in self-evaluation and determine your spending pattern. This will give you information to help you decide if you're spending excessively.

A lot of people see personal budget planning from a negative perspective. They see it either as a frantic attempt to avoid debt or some sort of handcuffs that prevent them from enjoying things that they want.

By looking at it this way, following a budget is only a necessary evil. However, it may be more helpful to focus on the long-term benefits that can come from the traditional budgeting process like composure and eventually, financial freedom.

Let's be honest. Most of us would rather spend as much money as we want without any limitations. It's in our nature to desire more for ourselves. Unfortunately, not all of us have infinite resources. So, choices are necessary.

3.4 Importance of Budgeting

Instead of tying us down, the act of making a personal budget is essentially a liberating exercise. It lets us make rational selections when it comes to our spending as we consider our entire financial picture. Incautious spending impulsively is traded by process of logical decision-making. It lets us prioritize our needs and desires in both short term and long term.

Without a budget, the money we worked hard for will have a tendency to go down the drain. A lot of people have a problem understanding why they don't have money left at the end of the month. Astonishingly, this happens not only to those who have low-paying jobs but also to those who have high-paying jobs.

If you're one of the people whose pay check doesn't stretch to cover each of your expenses, try to keep track of your spending for a month. Make sure you keep a record of everything you spend, whether by cash, credit cards, or check. You might be surprised how much money you spend on small purchases without having a second thought.

Extra Money for Long-Term Goals

Even more astounding is what you are able to save if you choose to get rid of those small, unnecessary purchases. If you take the money you'd have spent every month and put it toward settling your debt, you might be able to significantly lessen your number of payments along with the total amount of interest you need to pay.

Similarly, if your debts are settled and you want to save a bit of extra every month, you build up a considerable amount. For example, let's say you could save $100 every month by not having your coffee. If you were to invest that cash at a conservative 4% interest rate for more than a 40-year working career, you'd have more than $118,000!

This is only one example. When you look closely at how you spend, you might be able to find a lot of unnecessary expenses to get rid of.

By planning your personal budget, you are able to take control of your financial situation, instead of letting it control you. You are able to be in a place to substitute your instant gratification with the help of financial goals that need some time to achieve. Then, you are able to truly experience life without having to worry about your financial situation.

Learning *how to control spending and the use of credit cards* will mean the need to understand why you spend. If you are aware of the emotional reasons behind your spending, resisting it would be easier.

While the occasional shopping spree might seem harmless, the problem is that the effect of spending is so easy to underestimate. And, unfortunately, using words like 'shopaholics' makes it sound like it's a fun activity you can be proud of. But the effects hit you hard.

This spending indulgence normally comes with the use of using credit cards. It's a lot easier to give out the plastic and not dwell on what you're spending. What you have to know is that credit cards are essentially a loan that has to be repaid, and you'll pay interest on your loan balance.

You can take control of your use of credit card using the following steps:

- Plan your budget, taking note of all of your essential expenses like housing expenses, meals, and loan payments. Add other living expenses and subtract them from your income. You must know what's coming in and what's going out in order to know which changes you need to make. You need to be very honest with yourself.

- Add a credit card payment in your budget. This has to be more than the minimum obligatory.

- Have a notebook where you can record all of your spending you do for a couple of months regardless of how small the purchase. You will be amazed at how much you put out.

- When you go out, you may want to leave your card at home. Ask a reliable friend to keep it for you to control your spending.

- Choose to use cash. Think that if you don't have cash, then it means you can't afford it.

- Before you spend anything, make sure to think twice. Ask yourself if you need that item. Don't buy things impulsively, try to sleep on it.

Budgeting and emotions come hand in hand, so by controlling one of them, you are also affecting the other.

Chapter 4

Creating an Effective Budget

Whatever you are looking for in life, whether it is wealth, health, prosperity, love, or just success along the way, everything begins with your mind-set.

But can you even change the way you look at money? There are different tactics on how you are able to change your mind-set.

Our mind is extremely powerful, and when used the right way, you are able to change your life around. Keep reading to know how you can alter your perspective on the money with the following simple to follow steps.

Why Is It Important To Change The Way You See Money?

I grew up in a family that was struggling with money. Looking back, I blame my parents for having "just enough" to survive. Because their mind was set to: "as long as you have enough to get by, it's enough."

But I need to blame myself more for accepting this mind-set from them.

Of course, there are a lot of people out there who'd be very happy with having enough money to survive, especially the ones who live pay check by pay check. Having such a narrow perspective on money or about the abundance of money could hold you back in your life.

Try to look at it this way: having enough money is going to get you the absolute minimum. It may perhaps...

...settle the bills but not give you enough money to set aside.

…buy your meals, but not the pleasure of letting you try new dishes, eating out, or choosing healthier options.

…let you work very hard for your money but making you sacrifice time and passion.

…give you the chance to have occasional vacation but with limited funds and not enjoying the luxury of business class and 5-star hotels.

…make you survive but not entirely experience life.

You see, having enough can make you survive, but it wouldn't let you enjoy life to the fullest. This is going to cost money, and I believe that every one of us deserves to live our life the way we want.

That was one of the main reasons I felt unhappy and looked for something until my mind-set towards money changed. I was able to change it. And so can everyone!

Most people think that having the right mind-set is something you might or might not have; they think that it is something someone is born with, but that's not really the case. It is something you are able to learn and train, just like any skills or talent one could have. Here are some ways to train yourself to improve your relationship with money.

1. Forget all the things you learned as a kid

Well, I'm not talking literally everything, but in terms of our belief system, most of us have unfortunately usually gotten a completely wrong message.

I'm sure; as a kid, you heard an adult saying, "Money doesn't grow on trees."

Well, turns out I was not the cleverest kid; otherwise, I'd have told them that money actually grows on trees because they are used to make paper.

But that's not the point! The point is I believe that people like to use sayings like this too casually and don't really consider how damaging they could be to a young person's mind.

So, if you have kids who are too young to understand deep sayings or idioms, try not to use them. You can explain things better in simple words rather than confusing them.

2. Forget about your past

It's not just what others told you regarding money, but it's also about what belief system you made yourself.

I told you earlier how I unhappy I was in the past even though I earned a handsome amount of money. And if I were living the same way right now, I wouldn't be here in my situation right now. I wouldn't be where I wanted to be.

For example, I lost a lot of money on a business that failed many years back. It took me quite a while before I was able to recover. If I let it become my "new reality" – that I would just lose a lot of money if I start a business again, then I would not have a successful business at present.

Don't let your past define what you are now and what you could do in the future. One can always learn from his mistakes and can turn everything around if he wants it enough.

So, learn from your past, once you are done, leave it all behind and start a new chapter.

3. Change your money story

Forgetting something bad from the past might not be too difficult, but how about your present struggles?

If you're currently dealing with debts or in a situation that involves money, it's even more important to change your feelings about this immediately. It's going to be difficult to attract abundance and positivity when you're in a state of lacking.

But the good news is that you can trick your mind into the state of abundance, no matter what kind of situation you are in at present.

I'm not suggesting that you should maximize your credit card to afford to live in luxury even if you are about to lose your car.

But in case you don't have any debt you need to pay off, then why not?

What I'm saying is that don't live off the idea that you can't afford the good things when you know you could. Don't deprive yourself of the good things because you love money to the point that you don't want to spend it anymore.

Ask yourself – do you live to work, or do you work to live? Don't be afraid to spend your money on things that matter. This being said, you must still be careful about where you spend your money. A minimalist budgeter is not afraid to spend his money, but rather, afraid to spend his money on things that wouldn't bring him joy or improve his life in the long run.

4. Fake it until you make it

Once you got over the first three points, you can now proceed to talk to others regarding your situation as if.

I'm encouraging you to lie; in fact, please don't! You can just say something like, "I have a stable money situation right now; I'm aiming to work on my money mind-set, though."

What I meant by "fake it until you make it", is to make yourself believe the positive side all the time, even if it means you're not really confident with your money situation.

When you start telling your goals to people, you will be more motivated to prove to them that you are telling the truth. But please, don't put yourself in a situation where you will find yourself hanging by a thread. For example, although it might be your dream to buy a beach property on an isolated island, you don't have to tell them that you are already buying that property when you are not yet.

Always believe in your dreams and make them happen.

5. Make a vision board

When changing your mind-set, visualization is such an effective tool, and a vision board could absolutely help you throughout the process.

When you start taking advantage of a vision board, you would be amazed at how powerful the law of attraction is when it comes to changing your perceptions towards money.

On your vision board, start putting the amount of money you wanted to earn, you can change it as your earning shows signs of progress. And when you look back, you will see how the number changes over time.

This might sound very simple, but it could truly make a great change in your life.

6. Practice gratitude

What are the things you are thankful for?

Create a gratitude list or a journal and list down the things that make you happy on a daily basis. This method will show you the magic of the law of attraction.

At the end of the day, I write everything I am thankful for on that day, and it makes me realize how lucky I am for having my life. This exercise improves your overall mind-set and not just your mind-set towards money.

Try it out, and you will immediately see what I am talking about. Some people do this in the morning, while for me – like I said – I do this before I go to bed.

However, practicing gratitude is a lot more than simply writing down the things that make you thankful. Gratitude is something you must live the whole of your day, no actually your whole life.

You can start by being grateful for all the small things you have in your life, and I am 100% sure that no matter what situation you are in at the moment, once you start working on your gratitude, you'll find more and more things you will be happy about.

It's not going to take long until you realize that this is going to change your whole mind-set; your filter is going to be set to things you're grateful for, and you'll attract more good things.

7. Start to love money (but not too much)

Okay, this one should not be too difficult. But because this is something that is very important, I should add it to the list.

There's no way you can build a positive money mind-set if you have any negative feelings towards money.

There's nothing bad with being wealthy – in fact, it's a good thing!

I don't believe that money is the root of evil. It is the person who holds the money who is accountable for the evil things that are taking place! Some people look at money as power – power that they can use to general good things and bad things.

But money is not the culprit.

I mean, just think about the things money can do to improve people's lives.

Don't feel guilty for loving money. If you feel a little bit uncomfortable for having a lot of money while some people are living in poverty, then you can always help them.

You can always help people through charities.

Doing this will not only make them happy, but the sense of fulfilment knowing that you offered a good deed would make you so much proud of yourself.

So, if ever you have negative feelings towards money, try to turn them around, and think of all the good things you could do with it.

8. Be more confident

Many people underestimate what they are worth. But what they don't know is that it's one of the worst things they could do to themselves.

Everyone always has something to offer, and it's important for each one of us to focus on those things.

This could be raising the rate for your products or services or asking for a salary raise from your boss.

Never sell yourself short – you'll immediately realize that you're worth a lot and you deserve more than you are actually getting. You must be confident your time and skills are worth the money you want to have.

9. Set your goals high

The problem with some goals is that they're not big enough to keep you motivated to work on them.

Big goals can truly fire you up. So, in terms of money, it is even more essential that you're thinking big.

No matter what you can offer in the world to earn money in return, I'm sure that there's someone in the world doing the same and earning a lot more money than you can ever imagine.

I mean in today's world, it's almost normal to hear people doing these following things while earning a handsome amount of money:

- ❖ Helping people in need
- ❖ Traveling the world
- ❖ Sleeping
- ❖ Tasting food
- ❖ Staying at home

So don't you think it is time to think big and change how you see money?

Of course, there are more things you can do to change your mind-set from dearth to abundance. It's just all up to you how you can go about it. But I hope the tips are enough to help you get started without your shift.

4.1 7 Ways to Save Money with Minimalism

After finishing grad school, I was a complete mess. In debt and confused, you can compare my life as if I was climbing a mountain of problems without a clear vision of where it is going to end. Fortunately, I since have found a minimalist lifestyle. It allowed me to save money and create a plan on how I am should deal with my debt. Now, let me talk about the ways I used to save money through minimalism.

1. I fixed my hobbies

We live in a time where almost every possible hobby or pastime is within our reach. Gone are the days we need to drive to the nearest theater or rent tapes and CDs if we want to watch movies. We can literally browse hundreds of movies and watch them through our computer or even a smartphone.

For me, however, this excess of choice led to infinite indecision. There are too many options. Choosing has been a challenge. So, not only I wasted money paying for subscriptions, but I also wasted my time.

I thought hard about what hobbies I want to try and lock in the things that I truly enjoyed spending time on. I also tried looking for more activities that wouldn't require me to spend money. Some of those hobbies include riding my bike and hiking.

2. I consolidated my pantry

Same as the aforementioned situation, I had an ever-changing interest in different kinds of foods. I was not quite at the point where I was eating instant noodles every night, but I certainly had to watch my meal budget. What I did that certainly helped me the most was coming up with a weekly meal plan.

On Sunday evening, I would prepare a full set of meals for lunch, snack, and dinner. I normally used cheap ingredients like pasta or rice, and making tasty and healthy dishes with a great range of vegetables has saved me a lot of money.

I also saved tons of money by growing my own supply of some items that could be expensive. Basil, for example – a bottle of basil that I need to make 4 servings of pesto used to cost me $5. Sometimes I would not even use the entire container before it went bad. This spring, I planted basil plants together with some other herbs for about $10, which gives me enough for the whole summer.

3. I used fewer appliances

Many people I know have two or more refrigerators in their home. Some keep a lot of frozen food and such, which is understandable. However, there are others who simply need space for a great range of snacks and desserts.

My sister even kept two washers around just for the reason that for her, moving heavy things is so inconvenient. That's when I saw several problems with that. Not just do old appliances consume a lot of space, things like old refrigerators could have chemicals in them that could seriously harm the environment and even humans if not disposed of properly.

4. I tried thinking smaller

For me, this step came a little later in the process, and it makes sense that it did. When I came to a point where I had so many kitchen gadgets, a lot of hobbies, as well as wasteful appliances, I tried to convince myself that I needed a huge house in order for me to have enough room for everything I had.

But ironically, the moment I cleared up other parts of my life, I was more eager to move to a smaller space. And as I mentioned earlier, this also had a surprising effect on keeping me honest in my minimalist lifestyle. I control my impulse purchases with one question, "Am I going to have a space for this?"

5. I used my credit card carefully

I know how the use of a credit card is very convenient. I'm not going to tell you to stop using it completely. In fact, I did not even get rid of mine, and there have been times when it saved me from trouble due to its convenience.

Now, just focus on "used it carefully". This just means you have to be responsible every time you use it. I used it only during the times I REALLY needed it.

6. I changed my mindset

Every practical advice in the world will not help you if you do not adopt a great mindset. Today, I try to focus on the good things that I can do for myself and for others, and I mainly do it by decluttering. I have a basket in my garage where I put everything that I no longer want or need. I was able to get rid of a lot of clutter by doing this. I donated them, sold them, or just disposed them.

I know that from the outside, minimalist budgeting or lifestyle itself may look like a weird cult for others – I used to look at it this way. It included people who were not like me at all. I thought it minimalists are individuals who can easily give up and let go of a lot of things in their life that I couldn't even imagine doing back then. I have since learned that this is not the case at all, obviously. For me, a minimalist lifestyle is fueled by lifestyle changes and gentle attitude, by dealing with problems one by one with a positive and generous mindset.

4.2 Steps to Having an Effective Minimalist Budget

For many people, finance can be truly complicated… but the truth is, it doesn't have to be. With a bit of effort, you are able to simplify your financial life and eliminate all the financial headaches you might be facing.

I consider myself a minimalist, and that's why I try to shy from any forms of complexities. I try to do everything in the simplest way possible. I go for stress-free solutions – I try to do things simpler so I can focus on more important things in my life.

Now, let's talk about how I simplify my financial life.

I'm going to share with you a step-by-step guide on how I made a practical budget that helped me reach my financial goals. "Practical" would be the keyword here.

If you have soaring hopes, just like when I started budgeting, and you make your budget too restrictive, it's likely for you to be unsuccessful in this. What's worse is that you might begin to have a mentality that you are just not great with money. This is not true at all. Every single one of us can be smart with their money. I truly believe that money management has a lot to do about having the right combination of mind-set and knowledge. You are required to have knowledge in order to make a plan that makes your money work for you, and at the same time, you need the mind-set to effectively follow-through with your plan.

I haven't met any person who has reached their financial goals without any type of budgeting system. A budget is probably the most important step towards financial freedom and success. There are a lot of different ways to budget. Some would do bi-monthly budgeting, others would do monthly budgeting, and there are some who would even do it annually.

It's important for you to find what really works for you. This might be dependent on three different factors: your salary schedule, your regular spending, and what triggers your spending. If shopping has become your weakness when you're feeling stressed out, having a monthly budget instead of an annual budget will be ideal for you.

In my case, I get paid every 15 days, have to settle a couple of major expenses, and my weakness is night outs with my friends. I find that making a monthly budget worked best for me.

At first, I followed the bi-monthly budgeting. It was so difficult for me, and unsurprisingly, I failed to keep my expenses within my set budget. How did this happen, you may ask…

Well, let me give you an example of why. Okay, so I gave myself $80.00 for when I go out with my friends. Well, technically I gave myself $160.00 per month for when I go out with my friends, but since I split my month into two budgets, I had no flexibility with that spending.

Now, let's get into it – Here are the steps I took to deal with my current budget, which works very well for me, that I want to share with you in the hope that they help you with your own budget planning.

Step 1: Track Your Spending Every Day for a Month

It's so easy to find tips and advice online that suggests how you can track your spending for 3 months before creating a budget. However, if you are reading this, I'd be guessing that you probably don't want to wait three more months to start changing your budget. If you're really serious about generating a realistic budget, you can start tracking your spending right now. It doesn't matter if it's in this middle of the month – simply record all your expenses for the following 30 days and then begin your budget at the beginning of next month.

You can get a journal, but I just like using the simple "Notes" App on my smartphone to track all the things I need to document. Because I almost always have my phone with me, I simply fill this in whenever I have to spend money on something. If I'm in a rush, I would simply ask for a receipt or check my bank account to record them at the end of the day.

I like putting things in categories. I suggest that when you are tracking your daily spending before making your first budget, you may want to put your expenses in categories as well. It is easier to figure out what your categories will look like when all things are already sorted. For example, try not to put, "burger—$5.00." Instead, you may want to write "eating out—$5.00." It is going to make things a lot easier by the time you need to calculate your expenses.

If you are going to make a monthly budget, you may want to up your spending around two weeks into your budget tracking. If you think you are spending too much on something, then try to lessen that spending in the following weeks. By following this, you will have you a better sense of what expenses you can realistically reduce when you are making your first budget.

Since I make monthly budgets, I compute my spending in every category in the middle of the month. I am able to determine precisely what spending money I have left in every category I listed. I normally then write something very informal:

"As of March 15:

Groceries—$100

Transport—$90

Entertainment—$80

I have this information in my smartphone, again normally within the same note, so that I can easily look at it before I buy something.

Because I have gotten used to tracking my spending, it has become very easy for me. When it becomes a habit, it would literally take 5 seconds for you to take out your phone and write the information you need. It also literally takes not more than 10 minutes to review the categories.

Step 2: Know Your Fixed Spending

Your fixed spending is the expenses that you have to settle on a regular basis, usually every month. The items in this category include, but are not limited to the following:

- ❖ Rent
- ❖ Electricity
- ❖ Water
- ❖ Mobile
- ❖ Retirement Savings

As the minimum payment on your student loans is going to change as you are paying off your dues, you must eventually have an estimate as to what it is going to be.

Say, for example, the minimum payment last month was $250.00. Instead, you can make the minimum payment amount for your student loans $350.00. That way, in case it changes, you know you can cover it. But then again, you can simply check your student loan balance by the end of the month to identify the minimum payment before finalizing the budget for the following month.

Your phone bill might also occasionally vary. There might be some months when you could unintentionally go beyond your data limit and have to pay more the following month. It is not really a big deal, but you have to remember that when you are making the budget for next month.

While these are considered as "fixed" spending, you still need to make a budget for every single month. And even though you can normally just copy and paste these expenses when planning your budget next month, it's still important to go over each item, just to make sure.

Other things you may want to include under fixed spending are:

- Utilities
- Car Insurance
- Subscriptions (i.e., gym membership, Netflix)
- Insurance
- House maintenance
- The minimum payment for loans and debts

Step 3: Make Yourself Aware of Your Variable Expenses

These are expenses that you, usually, have more discretion over.

Here are some of the examples:

- Dining Out
- Coffee
- Groceries
- Entertainment
- Pet Supplies
- Transportation
- Healthcare

- ❖ Gifts
- ❖ Miscellaneous Fund

My category for grocery hasn't been changed for months. I usually change it when there are occasions when I have to prepare more food than the usual, like Christmas day, birthdays, etc.

"Personal Funds" are the funds I can use for personal expenses. I use this category when I have to pay for books, clothes, medicine, and anything I feel like treating myself with. Furthermore, if I have maxed out the budget for other categories, and I manage to have some left in this category, I would use this budget.

I find having a "Miscellaneous Fund" extremely important. This is basically an emergency fund for unexpected expenses. You never know what might happen! Although the following a strict budget is doable, there are still instances where you have no choice but to spend outside your planned budget categories.

Some of the things you might need this budget for are the following:

Car or Home Maintenance

Gifts for a special occasion

Someone has to borrow money

Unplanned donation

Step 4: Choose What to Do with What's Left

Okay, now it's time for you to do some basic math. Deduct the total amount of your fixed spending and variable expenses from your monthly net income and presto! That is the amount of money you are left with. Keep in mind that these remainders shouldn't be used to satisfy your leisure. Don't go spend them at a fancy restaurant or to watch a movie.

This money must strictly be used to support your bigger financial goals. You could add that money to the next month's emergency fund, or you could simply save it.

If you have debts to settle, then your number one priority to achieve financial freedom is to pay them off.

Also, if you have different goals like moving to a new house, a dream vacation, saving for a wedding, then you are able to use your discretion on how to split up this money. But then again, using this money on different random things can be a great mistake.

Step 5: Track Your Spending… Again

You are not done just yet!

You're probably wondering why I am telling you to track your expenses again after making a well-thought-out budget plan. But this time, I want you to do it again in order to see if it actually works.

At this point, tracking your expenses shouldn't be too difficult anymore and should not feel too burdensome. In the first month, using a new budget is the most important. By the end of the month, know what you think worked and what did not, and use that in making a new budget for the upcoming month. Honestly, it will probably take you about a couple of months before you sort out perfect budgeting. So, if you think that it didn't work for you the first time, don't give up just yet. Great money management may take some time and practice, so be patient and don't give up right away.

I don't think you need to track all your spending and expenses for the rest of your life, though. For many people I know, they recorded each of their expenses for months. When they already knew their budget as well as their spending habits, they stopped tracking their daily expenses regularly. This practice will surely give you a chance to develop a better sense of where you think you are at when it comes to spending, and when you are getting close to maxing out your set budget.

Breaking down of Budget by Percentage

What I learned is when you look at your budget by percentage, instead of numbers, it is going to be more convenient.

Here's the breakdown of my current budget:

Fixed Expenses: 32.89%

Variable Expenses: 46.02%

Remainder: 21.09%

But remember that we may have different incomes, so in order to look at and imitate what someone else spends is not going to benefit you. Ultimately, after calculating everything, I'd estimate that I'm roughly living on a little more than half of my income and the rest goes to short-term savings as well as a retirement plan.

As mentioned earlier, minimalist budgeting may not work the first time you do it. Actually, it did not work for me as well at first. I exceeded my budget plan for my first two months. That's when I knew I needed to change something in my approach. The following are the things I did in order to perform it successfully:

> ### I tried to avoid consumerism

This has been the first and most important step for you. Most of the time, it's so easy to set out the mind-set of buying or attaining more, to shop for pleasure or to relieve stress, or simply buying impulsively. This is a mind-set that roots from years of being exposed to advertising, and it's not easy to stop. You can start by becoming more aware of it and by telling yourself that you'll no longer find pleasure in getting and buying material things.

If ever you find yourself wanting to buy something so bad, sit back and take a deep breath. You can list it down and let days go by before buying it. Normally, the impulse will dispel. Think thoroughly about every purchase you make and ask yourself if you really need it or you can survive without it. Trying to live with a minimalist budget is trying to live only with things that are truly important and get joy from doing things.

> **I saved up for rainy days**

Before you reach financial peace of mind, it's important for you to have funds you can use for rainy days or times of emergency. Otherwise, you are always going to live on the edge, from pay check to pay check. Every unexpected spending that comes up will disrupt everything I'm recommending below.

You can get started here: Save up about $500 by putting aside $50 to $100 every time you get your pay check, and eventually build up to $1,000 or more.

In order to do this, cut out pointless expenses. Look carefully at the way you spend, including regular payments you may have forgotten about, and see what cut you can make. Some of these cuts may include the following:

- magazine subscriptions
- buying books (instead, borrow from libraries)
- cable TV
- more expensive mobile phone plan
- gourmet coffee
- a bigger home than you need
- storage space
- shopping for too much food
- too much entertainment that you can skip

Make the cut and put the money to you rainy-day funds. There shouldn't be a limit for how much you can save for this budget, but if you want, you can still have a limit of how much.

> I got out of debt

Debt payments aren't essential – well, you shouldn't have them in the first place anyway. However, until you have settled your debt payment, they are going to be a headache.

After saving at least $500 for your rainy-day fund, you can put off your extra income towards debt payment, one debt at a time, until you are all paid up. Perhaps put a bit on each pay check towards your rainy-day fund.

Last Piece of Advice

There's no shortcut in making a budget that you can stick to and that will work for you. A budget is, nevertheless, a breathable outline for your money habits. A budget shouldn't just reflect your present lifestyle but also be the main tool that is going to help you reach your bigger goals. On the other hand, if you already have all the things you might possibly need, then put aside that money for your emergency funds.

Other Important Things to Remember

Use it together with good budgeting tactics. You are able to use minimalism – and more mindful shopping habits – to make your budgeting skills better. However, practicing minimalism alone does not replace good budgeting methods. Figure out if you have enough self-control over your spending. Have you actually grasped the flow of money in your life? Do you have an idea where your money goes every month? These are important questions to answer when trying to improve your budget.

Learn how you can align minimalism with your long-term budget goals. Always look at the big picture. You want to ensure that you are also saving money for your future goals. It's important to make sure that your money is going to the right places; places where it will help you grow your wealth or get closer to where you want to be and what you want to have.

This just means that along with cutting down your expenses, you must also be putting your money on savvy savings and investments that match your long term and midterm goals. For example, if all your unspent funds are sitting in a no-yield checking account, you may consider moving them to a high-yield savings account, low-fee mutual fund, or certificate of deposit, depending on what your financial goals are.

Don't be afraid of your debt; instead, just be mindful about it. There are minimalists who preach absolute hatred towards debt, which includes student loans and mortgage debt. However, financial experts caution that there could be room for savvy debt management within your budget.

Yes, you must absolutely pay down high-interest credit card debt and think carefully before you take on new debt. However, the concept of leveraging money could be a really smart method to build your wealth. As long as you do it right, with the right kind of debt, you are good to go.

For example, getting the right amount of student loans, which could be an important investment for your career in the future – try to get no more than your expected first year's salary. Paying down a fairly low-interest mortgage aggressively might not make sense if you have more persistent financial goals, like putting up funds for your retirement savings account.

So, always think carefully before shunning all debt. These could be beneficial as long as you know how to manage them.

It's important to practice that same level of mindfulness in your financial life. As you reconsider your belongings to decide whether they add value to your life or you're better off without them, try the same practice with your financial accounts.

Do your retirement accounts still bring relevance to your life, or is it better for them to be rebalanced due to current economic and personal changes? Does your savings account still meet all the expenses you need to pay? Does the amount in your bank keep you happy and contented? Take a moment to reassess and re-examine the financial situation on which you rely so as to make your financial future happier.

Chapter 5

Budgeting for the Long Term

It seems that today, everyone has been talking about minimalism – it just has become a trend. From tiny houses to decluttering, to living with no more than a certain number of belongings, a minimalist lifestyle attracts people who are looking to change or improve something in their life. And as you know by now, minimalism is very beneficial for those who want to manage their budget on a long-term basis.

Budget to Your Heart's Content

Budgeting is the secret to saving money, regardless of what lifestyle you would like to have! By having a clear plan of you need and having a clear picture of the road to take, it's going to be easy for you to manage your budget as a minimalist in the long term.

Minimalist attitude is something we should have. This budget could also help you learn how to make the most of your budget, minimize your spending, and make your savings even bigger.

If you choose to ride a bike as your form of transportation to work, then you avoid spending on anything except for the bicycle itself, which you had probably paid for when you bought it, and its maintenance. If your mortgage or rent is a huge chunk of your money, maybe consider a smaller house, which means you might have to eliminate a lot of your "stuff" because you'll have limited room space. Even food could be minimized by growing vegetables and herbs, instead of buying them in store.

Follow Your Budget, or it is Pointless

How many of us have made a budget, followed it for a while, then ignored it completely? Pretty much almost every one of us! As mentioned earlier, it is not that simple to make the budget plan, and if we're feeling overwhelmed by it, looking at it again is something we are trying to avoid. But if you want better things to come, just follow it!

Spend at least 15 minutes every week to check your budget plan and make sure that you are on the right track. Yes, there are days when you will not be able to follow it. But it is okay; we're only human! But remember that the more we look at it, the easier it is for you to get used to it and for it to become a habit. Knowing that you can control your finance is super empowering and fulfilling. Just try it, and you will know what I mean!

Buy Things that Last

Of course, there are things that are only good for a while like food, clothing, etc. and that's alright. But there are many things that are meant to last for a long time. When you need to shop for something, you may want to focus on making sure that you're buying something that you can benefit from in the long run.

This might mean that you need to spend a little bit more money on it. The idea behind minimalist budgeting is not to avoid spending your money or being frugal but making the most of your money, whether it means you have to pay triple of the price of the cheaper version. Just imagine buying a microwave that costs $50 that would likely break down after a year of use, or even earlier. Do you think it's more worthy than its $150 version that comes with 5 years warranty? Invest in high-quality furniture, and you'll spend less as you wouldn't have to replace it every so often. It should always be quality over the price tag.

Choose What You Need, Not What You Want

If you don't know already… yes, there's a difference between what you need and what you want. It's so easy to get caught up in satisfying your desires for the latest gadgets or the nicest clothes. While these things are indeed necessary for day to day needs, they don't have to be the grandest things.

As I kept mentioning in the earlier part of this book, marketers love preying on people who are soft when it comes to persuasion, even leading us down the road of what they want you to buy. But with a minimalist mindset, you will be able to focus on what you need rather than what you want.

It's also worth noting that the things we own don't define *who* we are! While the way you wear clothes may reflect your personality, it doesn't really define what's inside you.

Budgeting as a minimalist for the long term is truly attainable, so it's truly worth a try. There's no denying that a lot of people are so used to not saving and getting by with the money they earn, overlooking the amount they are already spending on a normal day. This is why applying mindfulness in all aspects of our lives, including our financial life, is extremely important.

Chapter 6

Setting Your Financial Goals

Again, in case I haven't stressed it enough already: The intention behind minimalist budgeting is NOT to be more frugal but to eliminate excess spending on things that don't bring value to your life, or as Marie Kondo says it, "things that don't spark joy."

Setting your financial goals can be rather difficult, especially if you have not even mastered the basics of goal setting yet. While money seems to make many things twice as complicated for some, you don't have to worry; here are the tips that will help you set your financial goals successfully.

1: Be Realistic

No matter what kind of goal you are trying to set, it's very important to always be realistic. If you are earning a minimum wage and your goal is to save a million by the end of the month, that's not realistic.

I know I mentioned how you should dream big or set a big goal. But there should be a limit on how big your goal is. And if it's really your dream to earn a million, give a realistic timeline to yourself; otherwise, you are just putting stress on your life over something that is not practical with your current financial situation. And if that's the case, just how keen will you be to set your financial goal again and give it a try?

It's okay to start small. As soon as you reached that goal, you can make your way up to the bigger and greater goal eventually.

2: Decide Your Target

Of course, you must have a target amount as well as a target deadline. Be as specific as you can. When your goals are specific, you will have more chance to accomplish it earlier.

If you write that you want to be "rich", don't you think it's too vague? I mean, how rich do you want to be? Another thing I don't get is when people use the word "someday" too much. When is "someday" going to happen anyway?

When you don't commit to a number and a date, you're just giving yourself more reasons to fail or back out, even. And you're setting yourself to failure. If you are really serious about setting your financial goals, try to give your best.

3: Learn How to Budget

We've discussed this topic earlier, so I'm going to be brief on this one.

It is not only about choosing the number, it also has something to do with plotting your way to attain your main goal. And in all financial situations, budgeting plays a big part.

To successfully meet your set date and amount, learning how to add and subtract is essential. You must know which expenses must be maintained and which ones are to be eliminated.

Setting your financial goal should be easy as long as you follow the right path. Forget the people you know who weren't very successful in attaining their goals. Instead, focus on working hard and the possible outcome once you successfully reach your goal. There might be times when you feel tempted to change direction, but fight off those temptations and think of the reasons why you started all these things in the first place.

Chapter 7

DEALING WITH THAT DREADED DEBT

The day I had that realization that my old habits had floated up, I was at a mall with my wife, shopping for Christmas gifts. It was just a snap. I randomly had the question in my head that changed my life forever....

"Why do we have to give people new things to express our love to them?"

Sounds like a simple question, I know. But, why is that instead of taking them to the beach, spending time with them, giving them a hug, helping them with house chores... we give them gifts? Are material things more valuable than offering them our time? I mean at least money is something you can earn again, but time... it's something you can't take back. So, why does it seem like people would prefer to give their loved ones material gifts on special occasions?

If someone gave me a shirt for my birthday, would I really appreciate it more than if someone chose to invite me to go to the beach for that special day?

I realized that day that I should value time and experience more than materials things. The same day was the day I changed my spending habits forever. I no longer waste my time, energy, and space buying things that I know I don't need.

Minimalism is really about transformation.

If you choose to leave your possessions and turn yourself to the things that are more important, such as relationships, you are really committing to changing yourself.

You will then begin to see life differently and ask things from a different perspective.

That's what happened to me since that day at the mall. And I am extremely grateful to the universe for giving me this kind of realization I knew I needed.

Now, going back to the question... ***how can minimalism help you get out of debt?***

Everyone wants to get out of debt – I mean who would want monthly responsibility of paying back money, right? Well, the first thing you need to know is that you can make this happen, probably earlier than expected.

According to a magazine I was reading the other day, a lot of people actually just accept that they're going to be in debt, one way or another, for the rest of their lives – at least in the US.

But wouldn't it feel amazing to never get bills in your mailbox again? Can you just imagine?! Well, minimalism can help you make this happen.

Let's get this straight, though: there is no such thing as a get-out-of-debt card – changes are necessary in order to make this happen. And to do that, you have to manage your money better.

A lot of people are guilty of spending more than what they earn. Unfortunately, when you owe money to companies, you don't really own anything that you're paying them for. Just see everyone who fell in hard times and happened to lose their homes. The banks are the new owner of those properties now. Once you fall behind on your mortgage, it's only a matter of time until the bank grabs the keys from your hands.

Well, there are two things you can do about this.

First of all, you can cut your expenses, and the second thing is to find a way to increase the money that is coming in.

You're probably thinking, "If only it was that simple!" Well, sit down, relax, and think of all the things you spend your money on every single month. Make sure to include food, gourmet coffee, transportation, and monthly online subscriptions – not only the major bills you need to pay for. Now, list them all down and pick ones that you know you can live without.

The next step is to look at the things that might hurt when taken out, such as the internet, Netflix subscription, or eating out. Cut back to the basic internet and mobile phone plans and remove eating out completely and resort to just cooking at home. Prioritize the more important things.

Some of the things you are regularly paying for are conveniences that you basically don't need to get by.

Next is to figure out how you can make more money in order for you to pay off the debt you have accumulated.

You can start by emptying out your home of stuff that you no longer use or need. If possible, sell them to add funds toward paying your bills.

For many, having a side business has been their solution. The same thing worked for me. I was working full-time when I started an online business. I managed to make it work, thankfully. Now, I've been self-employed for many years, and there's no way I'm going to look back.

If you know how to sort things according to their importance, making decisions on what you need and what you don't becomes easier. And getting my priorities straight is one of the best things I learned from living minimally.

7.1 Using the Concept of Minimalism to Plan Your Personal Transformation

I hope my story has encouraged you to take a step toward the transformation you need. Otherwise, I suggest you to start observing people when you are in public places. Observe their behaviour as they shop for more material things. Just observe the excitement registered on their face as they make the purchase and walk out from the store.

And then just imagine how they might feel on the day they have to pay their credit card bills.

Is their purchase still worth it?

I'm confident to say that most of the time, it's not. Most of the things we buy are not worth putting yourself in that sort of financial trouble.

There are more things in life that are more fulfilling.

Minimalism helps us see more important things and encourages us to ask questions about why we feel like we need to collect more and more things and what are the possible outcomes for these actions.

There are a lot of reasons why people spend too much and accumulate too many things. But one of the main reasons is to fulfil their unmet needs.

Of course, it's important to buy certain things such as food, clothing, and shelter to secure our safety. But if what you're looking for is freedom and happiness, shopping and splurging thousands of dollars in debt is not really the right path to attaining freedom and happiness.

The truth is that true freedom comes from financial stability and security, as well as the nurturing and cultivating of personal relationships. And while commercials will argue that *"you can't buy happiness, but you can buy ice cream; and that's kind of the same thing,"* YES. Buying ice cream indeed boosts your mood at the moment. But would it benefit you for a long time? And just for the sake of argument, let me tell you that while ice cream can make some people happy when consumed, think about how it will affect your health if you choose to eat ice cream often to fill that *void* in you.

One of the best things you can do for yourself is to figure out what really triggers you to shop too much and over accumulate. And then use the answers to understand why and how it has stolen your opportunity to attain genuine happiness.

Instead of shopping:

- ❖ Work on strengthening and finding loving and meaningful relationships with people around you.
- ❖ Learn to be appreciative toward things you already have.
- ❖ Follow what genuinely makes you happy and not what makes other people happy.

Money and possessions give us false happiness.

Always be curious about your real motivations and use what you find to bring your life towards the things that make you feel free from the possessions, pressures, and emptiness that materialism brings.

7.2 Mistakes to Avoid When Dealing With Debt

When you're already drowning in debts, it's so easy to feel confused as to what to do about it. While there are a lot of approaches you can do to ease your struggles when paying off your debts, here are the most common mistakes you should avoid when dealing with debt.

- ❖ **Ignoring the debts**

Ignoring your debt is one of the worst things you could do. By letting your bills pile up, you will just accumulate more dues in the form of late fees and interest. What's worse, you might even end up getting sued, have your car reclaimed, or if you're renting a house, get evicted. Regardless of how terrible it might make you feel, you have to settle those bills and return any calls you get from your creditors. And, of course, you must create a plan for how you are going to deal with those debts.

- ❖ **Dealing with debts without enough funds**

It's very just silly to think that you could get out of debt without having a budget in writing to help you manage your spending and overall money. The truth is that there's simply no tool that is more important to good debt management than proper budgeting. It is the only way to guarantee that the right amount of money goes towards paying off your top priority debts without compromising your daily needs.

- ❖ **Falling behind on your payment**

If you fail to keep up on your car loan, there is a big chance that your car will be reclaimed. And this could happen without warning or anything even if you just missed a single payment. Just imagine having your car one day and losing it on the next. This gets even worse if you need your car to go to work every day. This is not only going to be inconvenient for you but also for the people who depend on you if you have a family.

❖ Paying Only Your Most Forceful Creditors

If you have multiple debts and your money is tight, don't choose to pay the most aggressive creditor first just because you are intimidated. Don't be forced to pay the creditors that hound you the most. Look at them equally. If you know one debt is better settled first than the other, then do it.

❖ Making Promises to Creditors That You Can't Keep

When you're getting confronted by a creditor about a past-due debt or discussing how you are able to catch up on past-due payments, don't make promises that you know from the beginning you can't keep. It's important to make decisions derived from your budget and income and not on what your creditor wants to hear.

❖ Refusing to Stop Using Your Credit Cards

While this is a no-brainer, many people still commit this mistake. Keep in mind that if you are already having issues with your credit card payments, it's smart to put those credit cards away so that you are not racking up even more debt. If you are considering buying something and you currently don't have enough money to pay for it, just try to forget about that item completely. If you want to avoid temptation, then always leave your credit card at home and have just enough cash with you when you need to go out.

❖ Taking Out a Loan against Your Home to Settle Your Debt

If you are struggling just to survive and have equity in your home, it could be very appealing to get a loan and putting your house as collateral. However, using your home as collateral to acquire a second loan is one of the worst ideas you can come up with. You could eventually find yourself in a place where you could not pay for both loans and would lose most of your valuable assets.

❖ Getting a Loan from a Non-Traditional Lender

There are actually for-profit credit agencies that are going to persuade you into borrowing money from them for you to get through your financial woes. Also, companies like that will make you believe that they are going to help you pay your debt. Don't deal with these non-traditional lenders, especially the ones that will require you to use your valuable assets collateral. It's so tempting to get a loan from one of these lenders. Make sure to read your paperwork carefully, and it is likely that you will find that these loans are very expensive source of funds and that their terms are essentially designed, so you'll end up losing the properties you used as collaterals.

❖ Choosing To Work With a For-Profit Credit Counselling Agency

There's just no reason to work with a credit counselling agency that's for-profit. These agencies have one purpose only, and that is to make as much money as they can. Because of this, it's hard to trust their recommendations and believe them that they want the best for you. Actually, some of the for-profit credit counselling agencies might tell you to do stuff that earns them money at your expense and could essentially get you into legal trouble.

❖ Asking a Friend or Relative to Co-Sign a Loan

If you cannot get a loan from a traditional lender like a credit union or a bank due to your financial problems, think very carefully before asking a friend or family member to help by co-signing for a loan. This is not a good idea because if ever you fall behind your dues, they're going to run after the co-signee. This means you're not only making a problem with money but also with your relationships with people that care about you.

7.3 Effective Strategies to Clear Debts

No matter how much your debt is and how long you have been struggling with it, you have to know that there's always hope. Here are some tips you can follow to get out of debt from a minimalist perspective.

❖ Get Professional Help

You can find a financial advisor who can help you. Yes, this might cost you some money, but you can look at it as an investment. On top of telling you how you can manage your finances better, they could also save you a lot of time. The process might be quite slow, and it might span several months. However, you have to realize that you can't repay a big debt overnight. Thorough measures have to be taken over the course of time in order to control the damage you bring to your bank account and earn enough money to settle your debt.

❖ Plan Your Expenses

I understand that some people may be averse to hiring a professional financial advisor, especially the ones who can't really afford hiring one. But don't you worry, as anyone, even you, who don't have any financial background, can surely plan out his finances as long as he puts his mind to it. This might require you to take a seat and compute your numerous expenses, and you might even be required to narrow your expenses down to a day-to-day level. It's suggested that you assign a day-to-day spending cap, but don't sacrifice too much and just eat packet ramen for every meal. You might not be able to always experience luxury, but you definitely shouldn't need to live like a tramp just to get rid of your debt.

❖ Don't Spend On Things You Don't Need

I don't know how many times I have said this in this book already. But at this stage, you shouldn't be spending on things you don't need right now, even though you think it's something that you might need later in your life. It's easy to see why, but you'll be amazed that some people will still spend a lot of money on items they don't need. And the reason behind this is actually kind of saddening – some people do this because they've already lost a lot and feel that they can no longer rectify the situation. So, they might as well go all out and enjoy life as much as they can. This mindset is very toxic. I really hope that you're determined in choosing the better way.

Chapter 8

VALUING TIME

Time is money. In fact, if you come to think of it, most of us don't only sell our skills to earn money, but also our time.

It might be a cliché you have heard many times before, but you know it's true. We may not receive the same opportunities in life, but we all get the same 24 hours in a day. Time is money, so we need to give value to time as we do to the money. In fact, treat it as more valuable because as I said earlier: money is something you can earn again, while time is something you cannot get back.

The idea of saying time is money opens up a whole range of relationships between our money and time. The time is possibly the easiest to theorize. Again, all of us have exactly 24 hours each day. What we don't have an idea about is when it is going to end. How we spend time highly depends on us. Money is a bit vaguer. Depending on where and when we were born, we start off in a given socio-economic situation. Then factors like opportunity and education all come in to shape us. All these, along with other bigger background factors such as current economic conditions at the time of our living, define to a great degree how much money we're going to have.

8.1 Time vs. Money

As humans, we are bound by two concepts, time and money. Every day, when we go to work, we're offering our time in exchange for money. Others have more money to buy other people's time. On the other hand, others choose to invest their money in order to make more and more money. No matter how you manage your time and money, you're falling into one of these categories:

No Time and No Money

A lot of employees fall into this category. There are people who have no control over their time because they are working. And at the same time, they don't generate enough money to become financially independent as they live pay check to pay check.

People under this category likely don't have any savings, so they will probably get bankrupt within a month or two after losing their job. These people don't have real financial stability and also very little time to enjoy their life.

No Time and a Lot of Money

People who are self-employed, professionals, as well as small business owners, generally fall into this category. They usually have more money than the previous category. However, they usually work twice the amount of time.

People in this category have extremely high stress levels and usually miss important occasions because their world revolves around only their work. Even though they have above-average income, they don't have a lot of time to spend outside of work.

A Lot of Time and No Money

People in this category are usually the ones who work part-time, are students, or those who live off social assistance. They generally have more time than the average small business owners or employees. The catch, however, is that they barely have money to enjoy their free time completely.

A Lot of Time and a Lot of Money

Those who fall within this category are the luckiest. The internet has opened a lot of doors to people that couldn't be enjoyed by many people decades ago. Most people who enjoy this lifestyle are those who work online and investors who have control over their time and their income. There are the lucky ones who enjoy true freedom from time and financial problems. Other people who may also fall under this category include actors, musicians, and writers who usually generate royalties for their works. Investing your time into things that are going to pay you bonuses over time helps you enjoy life with a lot of money and a lot of time.

If you are living in a developed nation, changing your lifestyle might be easier. However, even if this is that case, it will still take effort, determination, and planning to be successful at it.

8.2 How to Work Smarter Not Harder

Waking up at 5 o'clock in the morning every day, traveling for almost an hour to get to the workplace, spending 9 hours at the office, and getting paid for 8 was a norm to me a few years back. My father said to me, "Son, you should work smarter, not harder," as I called him one weekend complaining about how I was starting to hate my job.

How can we do this?

Here are some important ways of how you can work smarter rather than harder.

Plan your tasks before you even start them

Planning is one of the best ways to work smarter. Planning can be done before you go to bed at night. List down all the projects and tasks you need to do in the following days, weeks, or even months. After doing this, do a comprehensive review of each of the tasks, classify them based on their importance, and figure out how much time is needed to execute each item on the lists. This will make doing this a lot easier.

Learn how to delegate

Some things can just be too overwhelming to the point that you can no longer do them on your own. Delegating tasks to others would be the best solution for this. This method will effectively free up your schedule and allows you to do other things that are important.

Have strict deadlines and stick to them

There are major tasks that tend to be big and involving. Because of this characteristic, we're drawn to procrastinate and not to do them even if we could have done them earlier. This is a harmful habit. In order to work on such tasks in a smart way, just divide them into smaller, manageable tasks. And with that, you can work on them one at a time. By doing this, you can assure that you can focus on the tasks and you will end up with a high-quality result and of course, you will be able to finish them on time.

Learn to Manage Your Time Better

Time management is one of the critical skills you want to improve if you want to work smarter. Time management will help you assign specific periods of time to every task that you need to do. A part of time management is to learn how to eliminate all the distractions around you. This will allow you to focus more on the task at hand. Finally, avoid multitasking. People think that they are being productive when they multitasking, but it just gives an illusion that you're finishing more things when the truth is that you are just delaying the tasks.

Take a Break

Both your body and mind need a break, and this is a part of working smart instead of working hard. Working for too long can definitely wear you out and reduce your capacity to do the necessary tasks. This is one of the reasons why for some people, no matter how much they work, they still get little results from their hard work. Set at least 20 minutes of break throughout the day to freshen up your mind and recharge your energy. With a fresh mind and body, it is going to be easier for you to maximize the results of your hard work.

Working smart involves strategy and when done right, leads to high-quality work. Following the tips mentioned above can help you to change your working methods and make them even better. Not only will you accomplish more within a short period of time, but you'll also have higher levels of energy left by the end of the day.

8.3 Why Society Doesn't Value Time

Have you ever noticed how some people think that they have a lot of time to do whatever they want to do? And have you ever wondered why this is the case?

These are the same people who you usually find in situations where they need to ask you to lend a hand on a project or give them a hand to do something they claim to be very important. It's also very common to hear this popular line from them… "Don't they realize how much pressure I am under right now?"

If they only knew how to value time, they wouldn't get caught in this situation.

But the question is… why do some people don't value this non-renewable resource? It's simply because they have no idea how to value it. If you find yourself in this situation, then let me guide you about how you can/should value your precious time.

Remember: Life is too short to be wasted

What will you do when someone asks you to offer him 5 hours of your day in exchange of $20? Would you take it? If you love yourself, please say NO. The way you value time reflects how you value yourself. And you are worth more than that! You're worth being paid enough, so don't sell yourself short. You deserve all the gratitude you can get from offering someone your time.

Know your value and know how to treat yourself better. Keep in mind that you are worth more than just a few pennies.

Repeat that to yourself, actually, believe in it, and act like it! There is no other way to do this. While I can't really walk you through each step in the process, here are some tips you can follow so you can treat your time better to make the most of it.

Don't Be Late: Being late shows how you don't value not only your time but also of others.

Use Your Time Wisely: Every second is worthy. As much as possible, I try to stay occupied anywhere I am at any time. When I'm riding the subway, I would read books or the newspaper. I listen to podcasts when I'm in the shower. I read books until I fall asleep. I try to use my spare time for self-improvement, as long as it's convenient for me. For me, it's all about using every moment of the day in an efficient way.

Know Your Priorities: What are the important things you do? Scrolling down on social media and keeping updated with other people's lives? Browsing online to look for things to buy when you have work you have to finish? Learning how to prioritize is extremely important. Decide what matters most and do it first.

Avoid Making Excuses: Everyone hates this, yet many are guilty of this. Look, I know it doesn't feel good to be held up by traffic, which causes you being late and missing the meeting. But why didn't you leave home early enough to make it on time despite the traffic? Stop using any excuse to save you from your own mistake. Be responsible for your action and value your time as well as other people's time.

Size Doesn't Matter: No matter how big or small, everything makes a difference when working toward success, your objectives, or anything you want to achieve. Take your time to say thank you. Give your partner a kiss before leaving to work. Listen to the news while you are in the shower. Every little thing is important.

Concentrate on the Present: All the things you are doing right now are going to benefit you in the future. But if you don't give importance to the present, it's going to be easy for you to get stuck in the never-ending loop of *"I'll do it tomorrow."* But remember that tomorrow never comes; it's just another new version of today. So, do it now, and do your best.

Stop Procrastinating: This is probably the simplest yet the trickiest culprit for wasting a person's time. It's so easy to identify someone who is procrastinating, yet many people still don't do anything about. If you find yourself ignoring an important work-related task to read Facebook Newsfeed or scroll through your Instagram, then you have a problem, my friend.

Procrastination kills motivation, creativity, and it doesn't benefit you. Just step up, get rid of all the distractions that trigger procrastination, and do what you need to do. If you find this difficult, just think like this: When you focus on doing your job, you will be able to finish it early; you will have more time to do the things that distract you without feeling guilty for doing it.

Take Control: This is probably the most important one, so read this carefully. Your problems are your problems, so no one else but yourself has to be responsible and accountable for it. By letting someone else affect your life and take that control, you are making a big mistake. Make better choices. Your life, your rules. You do you. If you fail at something, it is okay – just try again until you become successful at it. Believe in yourself and believe what you are capable of. Never let other people degrade you or make you feel insignificant. Only your judgment is important.

8.4 Busy vs. Productive

Day after day, it seems like the society and its people are becoming busier and busier than ever – which is kind of ironic as we are progressively creating new technologies that are supposed to give us convenience. Today, it seems like no one can find "free time" to do anything. It's a norm to run late for meetings, grab a meal on the go, and spend extra time at work. It's just so hard to keep up.

The most efficient and productive people are the ones who know how to own their day. They work hard in maximizing their time in order to be as productive as possible, not just to be occupied to do something.

The quest to be more efficient at work has emerged from the misconceptions about what having a productive workday really is. It has also made many people think that being busy is equivalent to being productive.

But the truth is that there is a huge difference between being busy and being productive. I spent years saying "yes" to all the opportunities that came my way and occupying myself with things that I can barely handle. But fortunately, I got to a point where I broke up my relationship to being busy and was able to introduce myself to being productive.

The Difference between Busy and Productive

Busy People	Productive People
Want to look like they have a mission	Always have a mission
Have many priorities	Have few priorities
Say yes quickly	Think hard before saying yes
Focus on action	Focus on clarity before action
Keep all doors open	Limit access to their doors
Talk about how busy they are	Let their results do the talking
Talk about how little time they have	Make time for important things
Aim for multitasking	Focus on one thing at a time
Make rushed decisions	Take their time for quality results
Always talk about wanting to change	Make necessary changes

Benefits of Stopping Being Busy and Becoming Productive

When you finally break up your toxic relationship with being busy, here are the benefits you will be able to reap:

You will make better projects. You will have enough time to create project-based learning unit plans and resources since you will no longer spend a crazy amount of time doing a simple task.

You will be inspired to take creative risks. When you find the root cause of working too much, you will be inspired to do things you didn't imagine you were capable of. Because you will have more time for yourself when you are productive, you will be able to have enough time to focus on your passion.

Your important skills will be improved. You will be able to figure out the skills you want to focus on. You will learn the things you are really good at and will have the chance to improve them if you choose to.

You will learn the importance of clarity. Productivity leads to clarity, the bluntness of expression, and purpose. It improves your ability to have a clear description of what has to be done, why it's important to do it, and how you can do it right.

You will have a work-life balance. The most important benefit of being productive is that you will have more time in your hands to do other things you personally enjoy. You can attain work-life balance when you're clear about your goal and know how to stay focused on things you need to do. This abolishes the pointless activity that gives you stress and causes fatigue. Furthermore, it will give you more time to do things you truly enjoy.

8.5 Productivity and Minimalism

One thing that many people don't realize is how minimalism plays a big part in our productivity. A study published by Microsoft Canada in 2015 concludes the following:

Canadians' ability to filter out distractions is a function of their surroundings, not their demographics, media consumption, social media use, or device usage. People with higher selective attention appear to actively choose to have fewer distractions and multi-screen less frequency.

This means that one of the differences between people who can keep attention longer and others who can't is that they intentionally generate a setting with fewer distractions.

The connection the study is talking about is not that complicated to understand. This just means that less use of gadgets, less noise in your environment, fewer tasks you commit yourself into, and less multitasking you do, cannot only initiate faster results but also better results.

What many people don't realize, however, is that productivity shouldn't be measured by the *quantity* of work you finished but the level of *quality* you achieved carrying out a task. The metric is no way centered on speed of production, but the level of quality.

The metric to assess the level of your productivity isn't how many things you did within the given time; it is how well you did in the process.

I believe that a minimalist approach to productivity is important to generate a helpful environment for better focus.

This includes:

- **Uninstalling all social media apps on your phone.** If you're really dying to check other people's lives on social media, then make it a little more inconvenient by using your mobile browser or use your computer. Perhaps, that little inconvenience makes you feel uninterested in checking social media accounts anymore.

- **Turning off the notifications on your phone.** Unless you are waiting for an important call or text, it's best to turn off your phone's notifications for when you receive calls, texts, or any alerts from any apps on your phone.

- **Using a small paper as your to-do list.** It's just that when you have a bigger paper to use or unlimited space on your app to create a to-do list, it's so satisfying to fill it up with tasks. So, the use of a small paper that can hold all the most important to-do lists would be a great option.

- **Disconnecting the internet when it's not needed for work.** It's just so easy to click on your browser and check out something for a few minutes. But most of the time, those " few minutes" turn into hours of time being wasted.

- **Listening to calming music.** Whenever I work, I become more focused when I'm listening to instrumental music, while for some, classical music or just white noise works better.

- **Cleaning your workspace**. Clutter and too much stuff around us can be so distracting. So, before working, cleaning your surrounding beforehand would be a good idea.

Since I am either writing or running my business almost every day, these simple strategies have helped me improve the overall quality of my life: I plan fewer daily activities, I learned not to care much about social media, and I learned many things that I truly enjoy outside the internet.

The spill-over effect of using a minimalist approach to improve my productivity has blessed me with a delightful surprise and has led me to reap the benefits of minimalistic lifestyle more seriously. It keeps reminding me that a state of overwhelm is mainly self-induced and could easily be managed through self-control.

Conclusion

Minimize, minimize, minimize.

We live in a world that can be so complicated. We are always so busy in a world that is so noisy and very distracting.

In order to counter that overwhelmed feeling, there is a movement happening in today's age, which persuades the idea of living a minimalistic lifestyle.

This might mean living with less, buying less, and owning less. Learning how to give importance to quality over quantity is one of the best things you could do with your money. Yes, it might be hard at first, but once you learn the benefits, it will come naturally.

Yes, I put up this book sounding like I know everything about managing your budget with minimalism. However, keep in mind that just like you, I had never really learned how to manage my budget before. It was pretty difficult to manage my funds. One important thing to remember is that it didn't happen overnight – I spent countless hours to successfully master what I preach. It was a process full of trials and errors.

I hope that this book has been helpful and gives you an idea of how to manage not only your budget but also your time. Furthermore, I hope this book encouraged you to take a step back and evaluate what you really need to live a rewarding life; you can spend considerably less.

Minimalism is not a synonym to being cheap – you don't have to count pennies or deprive yourself of necessities in order to create more wealth. Rather, eliminating your excessive spending helps you have more money to spend on things that matter more.

In my case, following a minimalist lifestyle has greatly liberated my funds, which I can use for following my dreams and fulfilling my goals. At the end of the day, my best source of wealth hasn't been measured in currency, but rather in the time and opportunity that I now enjoy living with a lifestyle that I genuinely love.